Negotiation

For James

If you've ever woken up feeling like the Jedi Master of sales one day and a stressed-out sweaty mess the next, welcome to my world.

It's a place where closing a deal can feel like a grand, triumphant victory… until the next phone call reminds you that you're only as good as your last sale.

But fear not—this book was born to guide anyone who's slogged through merciless targets, lazy bosses and a ruthless managed IT industry (yes, to my ex-manager, I'm looking at you).

After 15 years peddling everything from Apple products to Peloton subscriptions (with a dash of cold, corporate cynicism in between), I've seen it all—and most of it wasn't glamorous.

A million-dollar deal might make headlines, but the unsung heroes are the small, tough sales that demand genuine effort and sincerity. Why? Because smaller businesses aren't fooled by flashy demos or glossy brochures. They want a real person who rolls up their sleeves, understands their challenges and cares about their success. That's where this book comes in, offering practical tips, hard-earned experience and a little comic relief for those long days when you'd rather watch paint dry than dial another prospect.

Truth be told, this isn't just for you; it's also for my little boy, who I cherish more than life itself. While I secretly hope he'll dodge a sales career, the skills inside these pages—listening, empathy and resilience—will help him in any path he takes. Writing this has been unexpectedly therapeutic, a chance to exorcise the demons of a punishing schedule and a bully of a manager and transform them into lessons that prove we can come out on top, despite the odds.

So, grab a seat. By the time you finish this book, you'll be armed with the know-how to not only endure the madness but thrive in it. Discover how to make those tough sales as satisfying as striking a gong in a triumphant final moment.

Cheers,
Aidan.

1. Introduction: The Art and Science of Negotiation

2. Understanding the Psychology of the Buyer

3. Preparation is Everything: Research and Strategy

4. Building Trust: The Foundation of Successful Negotiations

5. Mastering the First Contact: Setting the Tone

6. The Power of Active Listening

7. Finding Common Ground: Aligning Objectives

8. Overcoming Objections: Turning 'No' into 'Yes'

9. Creating Value: Shifting the Focus from Price to Benefits

10. The Power of Silence: Using Pauses to Your Advantage

11. Reading the Room: Body Language and Non-Verbal Cues

12. Anchoring and Counter-Offers: The Numbers Game

13. Navigating Deadlocks: Staying Calm Under Pressure

14. Negotiating in Competitive Situations: Outmanoeuvring Rivals

15. Closing the Deal: Timing and Tactics

16. When to Walk Away: Knowing Your Limits

17. Maintaining Long-Term Relationships: Winning Beyond the Sale

18. Remote Negotiations: Techniques for the Virtual World

19. Negotiating as a Team: Leveraging Collective Strengths

20. Dealing with Difficult Personalities: Handling the Toughest Buyers

21. Case Studies: Real-World Negotiation Success Stories

22. Common Pitfalls to Avoid: Lessons from Experience

23. The Role of Ethics in Negotiation

24. Refining Your Skills: Continuous Learning and Improvement

25. Conclusion: Mastering Negotiation for Sales Success

1. Introduction: The Art and Science of Negotiation

Negotiation in sales is the process of creating agreements that benefit both seller and buyer. It is not only about finalising deals. Instead, it involves recognising everyone's needs and finding answers that bring genuine gains for both sides.

Good negotiation begins with solid preparation. You must know your own goals, understand what the buyer wants and remain open to different possibilities. Yet even the best plan can fail if communication is poor. Successful negotiators listen closely, ask meaningful questions and share ideas clearly to build trust.

Psychology plays a large part in negotiation. Observing body language, noticing emotions and making buyers feel heard is vital. These skills help you deal with objections and turn setbacks into new chances.
Remember that the best outcomes should help both sides. If one person feels cheated, the agreement may fail later, or the relationship may be harmed. A well-planned negotiation builds trust and sets the stage for future cooperation.

For those working in sales, negotiation is a key skill. It allows you to meet your sales goals while keeping customers satisfied. By focusing on preparation, communication and an awareness of human behaviour, difficult talks can become moments for everyone to succeed.

Negotiation also ensures that deals address the buyer's needs while meeting sales targets. It is not about taking just any offer; it involves finding the right deal so both groups benefit equally.

Each buyer is unique, with different needs, problems and budgets. Without negotiation, you risk presenting solutions that do not match what the customer really wants. Good negotiators ask questions, pay attention to the answers and adjust their offers to fit the buyer's situation. This helps build trust and shows clear value to the customer.

Negotiation is also important when juggling different demands. Sales teams must meet quotas, but pushing for a quick close can cause mistakes. By thinking carefully during talks, you can meet both the customer's requests and the business' targets. This might involve offering flexible options, crafting special payment plans, or giving long-term value.

Handling objections is another major part of the process. Buyers often worry about costs, deadlines, or potential risks. Skilled negotiators address these doubts in a direct way, which can turn concerns into stronger customer relationships.

In a competitive sales setting, effective negotiation helps top performers stand out. It leads to better deals, stronger relationships and happier customers. By matching buyers' needs with business aims, negotiation changes quick transactions into positive connections that last.

Some people assume that successful negotiators are born with the gift or that negotiation always revolves around price. These ideas often stop salespeople from improving their abilities.

The belief that negotiators are born, not made, is simply untrue. While confidence can help, research shows that practice and good preparation truly

lead to better results. Anyone can learn to listen carefully, use open-ended questions and handle tough conversations with the right training.
Another common mistake is to think that negotiation is all about money. Although price comes up, it is rarely the only concern. Buyers care about value—how a product or service solves problems or achieves goals. By highlighting benefits like quality, reliability, or future savings, you can shift attention away from just the cost.

Understanding these myths encourages salespeople to approach negotiations with a healthier mindset. It is not about natural ability or cutting prices again and again. It is about preparing, knowing your customer well and building genuine value.

Negotiation mixes both creativity and evidence. It takes intuition and the ability to adapt, along with reliable data and proven methods.
The creative side of negotiation involves sensing emotions, adjusting on the fly and connecting with a buyer. If a buyer hesitates, a perceptive negotiator might change the topic to uncover the cause of their worries. Telling a short story or sharing a personal example can also inspire a stronger emotional link to the offer.

The more structured side of negotiation focuses on preparation. This includes researching the buyer, working out their needs and listing the likely objections. Tools like the Best Alternative to a Negotiated Agreement (BATNA) help you gauge your position and past data can show which path to take.

Effective negotiators join these two parts together. A well-thought-out price plan may seem ideal, but if you notice the buyer values a long-term partnership, you might offer extra benefits instead.
By uniting flexibility with planning, you can create solutions that work and feel more personal for the buyer.

This book will show you how to master negotiation in sales. It offers practical tips for thriving in competitive markets.

You will first look at how buyers think. You will learn about what drives people's decisions, how emotions like fear and hope affect behaviour and how certain biases can shape actions. You will also find ways to spot different buyer personalities and match your style to theirs.
Next, you will learn the value of planning. You will explore how to research your customers, predict their concerns and set up a simple strategy before negotiations. Real examples and clear tools will help you use these ideas right away.

Building trust is another big theme here. You will gain methods for showing warmth, creating credibility and holding onto honesty in every chat.
There will also be specific advice on handling objections, shifting conversations from price to overall value and using advanced methods like silence or being mindful of body language. Case studies and stories from real deals will bring these lessons to life.

Whether you are new to sales or aiming to improve your skills, this book will help you build confidence, close deals everyone feels good about and earn long-term connections. You will find strategies for listening actively, dealing with objections and guiding the discussion away from cost alone. You will also study advanced techniques like noticing nonverbal signals and managing differences in power.

Filled with case studies, lessons from tricky situations and guidance on building your skills, this book gives you the tools to succeed in sales negotiations. Whether you have years of experience or you are just starting, you can use it to reach your sales goals while building lasting success.

2. Understanding the Psychology of the Buyer

Understanding why people buy is vital for success in a competitive sales environment. Buyers have two main types of motivation: **intrinsic** (coming from within) and **extrinsic** (coming from outside factors). When you recognise these motives, you can offer solutions that truly matter to them.

Intrinsic Motivators

Intrinsic motivators are personal reasons that drive buyers to act. They might want to solve a specific problem, achieve a personal goal, or feel proud of their decision. For instance, a company could choose a cybersecurity system not only to follow rules but also to protect its reputation.

To uncover these deeper motivations, try asking open-ended questions such as, "What are your main challenges?" or "What does success look like for you?" This approach shows empathy and helps you learn what truly matters to them.

Extrinsic Motivators

Extrinsic motivators include cost savings, increased efficiency, or gaining an edge over competitors. For example, a school may select a cloud-based IT system because it is affordable and simple to use.

When appealing to extrinsic drivers, focus on facts and figures. Share case studies, data, or return on investment (ROI) estimates that show how your solution makes a real difference.

Maslow's Hierarchy in Sales

Maslow's hierarchy of needs can help you understand what buyers want most. It has different levels that also apply to business needs:

1. **Physiological and Safety Needs**: Basic items like IT infrastructure or tools that reduce risk.

2. **Belonging and Esteem Needs**: Products or services that boost teamwork, brand image, or customer satisfaction.

3. **Self-Actualisation**: Transformative solutions that fit long-term goals or personal visions.

A good example is a Customer Relationship Management (CRM) system. It can improve day-to-day operations (safety), strengthen team cooperation (belonging) and support long-term growth (self-actualisation). When you meet more than one level of need, you build stronger trust with buyers.

Three Decision-Making Styles

Most buyers make decisions in one of three ways: **analytical**, **emotional**, or **intuitive**. Each style needs a different selling method.

- **Analytical Buyers**: They rely on facts and data. Offer evidence like case studies or detailed cost comparisons. Give them time to think. Do not push too hard or you risk losing their trust.

- **Emotional Buyers**: They focus on feelings and personal values. Share stories and testimonials that show how your solution helps people. Avoid drowning them in numbers.

- **Intuitive Buyers**: They see the big picture and decide quickly. Provide a simple explanation of the main benefits. Be ready to answer questions, but do not overload them with details.

When you adjust your approach to match each style, you show emotional intelligence and become a trusted adviser.

Fear of Loss and Desire for Gain

People often act based on two strong emotions: fear of loss and desire for gain. Understanding these can help you connect with buyers on a deeper level.

- **Fear of Loss**: Most buyers do not want to lose what they already have. Point out possible risks, like lost revenue or harm to their reputation, to create a sense of urgency. For example, emphasise the danger of a data breach to prompt quick action.

- **Desire for Gain**: Buyers want to improve their status, become more efficient, or earn higher profits. Show how your solution meets these goals. For example, explain how a new CRM system can improve productivity and give them a competitive edge.

Make sure you balance these two forces. If you talk too much about risk, buyers may feel overwhelmed. If you focus only on gains, they may not see the urgency to act. A balanced message—"Protect what you have while unlocking greater potential"—often works best.

Addressing Resistance

Buyers may resist your offer, but this does not always mean "no." It can highlight concerns you need to address.

- **Budget Constraints**: If a buyer thinks your solution costs too much, show how it pays off in the long run. Demonstrate return on investment and lasting benefits.

- **Lack of Trust**: Buyers must trust both the product and the salesperson. Build trust by being honest, clear and showing evidence like testimonials or measurable results.

- **Fear of Change**: Many organisations have established processes and worry about switching. Reassure them by showing how easy it is to start using your solution and what support you provide.

- **Unclear Priorities**: Sometimes buyers are not sure how your solution fits their main goals. Ask questions to discover what matters most to them and then link your product to those priorities.

By handling resistance with empathy and information, you can turn doubts into opportunities to prove your value.

Using Cognitive Biases Ethically

Certain cognitive biases influence how people see information. If you use them wisely, you can help buyers make better choices without being manipulative.

- **Anchoring**: The first piece of information sets the stage. Lead with the value of your best offer before talking about price. This helps buyers see its true worth.

- **Reciprocity**: People often feel the need to give back when they receive something. Offer helpful resources or insights, like an industry report, to show goodwill. Make sure it is genuine and free of hidden motives.

- **Loss Aversion**: Buyers are more motivated to avoid losses than to gain something of equal value. Politely remind them of the risks of doing nothing, such as missing a chance to grow. However, do not overstate the danger.

When used with honesty, these tools help buyers make wise choices and build strong partnerships for the future.

By understanding buyer motivation and behaviour, you can turn objections into conversations, create lasting trust and find success—even in tough sales situations.

3. Preparation is Everything: Research and Strategy

Preparation is the bedrock of every successful negotiation. Imagine stepping into a discussion without knowing where you're headed—it's like sailing through rough seas with no compass. You might know your end goal, but you also need a clear plan, backup options and the right tools to handle surprises.

In sales, preparation starts with learning about your customer. This involves studying their business, industry, challenges and goals. When I worked on a public sector framework agreement for the Royal Armouries, I spent weeks carefully analysing the tender documents. I also looked at trends in procurement and researched my competitors. This helped me craft a proposal that solved their problems and showed I understood their needs. Even with strong competition, we secured the deal.

It's just as important to know your own position. You should be clear on your profit margins, your limits and your alternatives. During a negotiation for a multi-site cloud solution, I knew the client might be worried about costs. So I arrived with data about long-term savings and different configurations that suited their budget. Because I was prepared, I stayed calm and flexible and the talk stayed friendly instead of turning into a fight.

Preparation isn't just about facts and numbers—your mindset matters too. Visualising a positive result, rehearsing key points and guessing what the other side might ask can turn a tense situation into a chance for success. A client once told me, "It felt like you knew exactly what we were thinking." That was not luck; it was the power of preparation.

Good negotiators don't rely on random guesses. By preparing fully, you gain the confidence to face challenges and turn them into good opportunities. Preparation makes strong deals possible.

Know Your Buyer and Their World

Success in sales begins long before you send that first email or pick up the phone. One step that many overlook is understanding the buyer and their organisation. In a crowded marketplace, this research can decide if you win or lose a deal.

Identify Buyer Needs

The best research starts with looking at what your buyer truly needs. Today's buyers are often well-informed. They expect sales professionals to share fresh insights. Start by examining their role in the company—their responsibilities, their obstacles and their main goals. A quick look at their LinkedIn profile can reveal their work history, recent posts and special interests. This helps you tailor your message so it matches their concerns.

Think about what keeps them awake at night. Are they trying to hit hard targets? Do they need to guide a team through sudden change? If you understand these worries, you can offer your product or service as a clear solution.

Investigate the Organisation

Next, dig deeper into the organisation itself. Read their website to learn about their mission, values and any new updates. Public companies usually share annual reports that highlight their main priorities. If the firm is private, you might find news articles or industry reports that help you see where they're heading.

Aim to match your product or service with their main goals. For instance, if they plan to expand into new markets, show how your solution can grow with them. Being specific shows you care about their success and have done your homework.

Analyse Industry Trends and Competitors

Knowing the buyer's industry makes you stand out. Ask yourself: What are the latest trends or breakthroughs in their field? Are there new rules or laws that could affect their work? By sharing these insights, you position yourself as a trusted adviser, not just another salesperson.

Also, keep an eye on their rivals. If you know what the competition offers, you can explain how your product offers something better. Maybe it's improved efficiency, lower costs, or happier customers. Either way, you show you can help them outshine the competition.

When you do strong research on your buyer and their organisation, you show that you're not just pushing a sale—you're fixing a problem. That's how you win in a challenging market.

Set Goals and Know Your Limits

Clear objectives are vital for effective negotiations. You need to know what you want, especially when the stakes are high. One popular way to set goals is using the SMART method: Specific, Measurable, Achievable, Relevant and Time-bound.

- **Specific:** Spell out your goal. Instead of saying, "I want to close a deal," say, "I want a three-year contract worth £50,000 each year."

- **Measurable:** Make sure you can track progress. For instance, "Have five client meetings and secure two signed agreements."

- **Achievable:** Aim high, but be realistic. If you pick unreachable targets, you'll likely feel frustrated.

- **Relevant**: Link your goals to your company's larger aims and the client's needs. Selling a high-margin product won't matter if the client cares only about low costs.

- **Time-bound:** Give yourself a deadline. For example, "Finish negotiations by the end of Q1." This creates urgency for everyone involved.

Along with SMART goals, be clear on your non-negotiable's, such as your lowest price or payment terms. At the same time, remember that flexibility often matters. You may need to adapt so both sides feel satisfied, but you should not give up on what truly matters.

Handle Objections with Confidence

Objections happen in most sales talks. Prospects often worry about price, timing, or whether your solution really fits. If you expect these concerns in advance, you can address them calmly and win trust.

- **Price Objections**: Some buyers might say your product costs too much. Show them the value you bring by sharing data, case studies, or proof of return on investment.

- **Timing Objections**: You might hear, "Now isn't a good time," or "Check back next quarter." Link your solution to their immediate goals to show why waiting might cost them money or miss a key opportunity.

- **Fit and Scepticism**: Sometimes buyers doubt your solution's effectiveness. Reassure them with testimonials or by offering trials or demos. Real-world success stories can ease their fears.

Focus on building trust by listening carefully. Position yourself as a trusted partner, not just a salesperson. When you answer objections with empathy and preparation, you turn them into reasons for your buyer to say "yes."

Create Your Pre-Negotiation Playbook

Preparation is so important that it helps to have a pre-negotiation playbook. This is a simple but powerful guide to ensure you're ready for anything. Over time, you can add new details to your playbook, refining it with each experience.

- **Understand the Customer**
  - Look at their business, industry and any major developments.
  - Identify their main challenges and their idea of "value."

- **Set Objectives**
    - Know your ideal outcome and what you can compromise on.
    - Consider wider goals, such as booking a follow-up meeting or strengthening the relationship.

- **Anticipate Challenges**
    - Prepare for common objections and plan your replies.
    - Think about their leverage, like budget limits or rival offers.

- **Build Your Strategy**
    - Sort your possible trade-offs and list what you cannot give up.
    - Prepare opening offers that set a positive tone.

- **Gather Supporting Data**
    - Have case studies, metrics and testimonials ready.
    - Know your numbers so you can talk about prices and costs with confidence.

- **Plan Roles and Communication**
    - Assign tasks to each team member, such as who leads and who observes.
    - Decide how you'll present your value.

- **Practise Scenarios**
    - Role-play mock negotiations to spot any gaps.
    - Adjust your approach based on what you learn.

With a solid playbook, you'll walk into negotiations feeling prepared and steady. Over time, you'll update this guide, turning each challenge into a chance for growth in the competitive world of sales.

4. Building Trust: The Foundation of Successful Negotiations

Trust is more than just a good quality in sales—it is a vital asset. Have you ever thought about how trust can speed up decisions and reduce doubts? When people trust you, they are more willing to follow your advice because they believe you want what is best for them.

Trust acts like oil for the sales process, helping things run smoothly. Without it, every discussion feels like a struggle, with clients questioning your motives. With trust, they move from asking, "Should I work with this person?" to saying, "How quickly can we get started?" This shift saves time and leads to easier partnerships.

Trust also creates emotional value. When clients trust you, they are less likely to argue over price or worry about every tiny detail. Instead, they work with you towards common goals. This builds stronger relationships and reduces how often you must search for new clients. By investing in trust, you clear a path for faster deals and steady, lasting success.

Building rapport is an important skill in any competitive field. If people feel noticed, appreciated and understood, they are more open to hearing what you have to say. Two helpful techniques for creating rapport are finding common ground and mirroring behaviour.

Finding Common Ground

Finding shared interests or experiences is one of the quickest ways to connect with someone. People are naturally drawn to those they see as similar to themselves. This can be as simple as sharing a love for a local football club or chatting about a mutual dislike of cold, rainy Mondays. Sometimes, you might notice clues in someone's office, like a particular book or a hobby displayed on a poster.

Ask open-ended questions to discover these connections:

- "I spotted that historical fiction book on your shelf. Are you a keen reader?"

- "You have a wonderful view here. Do you enjoy working in the heart of the city?"

Once you find something in common, use it to build trust and friendship. Remember, though, to keep it genuine. People can tell when you are not being sincere, which can push them away instead of drawing them in.

Mirroring Behaviour

Mirroring is another powerful way to connect. It means gently matching someone's body language, tone, or pace of speech. For instance, if a prospect talks calmly and slowly, speak in a relaxed way. If they are energetic, let your voice and energy rise to meet theirs.

When done naturally, mirroring makes both sides feel at ease. It helps create a friendly atmosphere where ideas can flow freely. But remember not to overdo it. If you copy someone too closely, you may come across as fake, which can harm trust.

Establishing credibility is just as important as building rapport. People need to be sure you can solve their problems. You can prove this by using your credentials, data and experience in a way that truly speaks to their needs.

Credentials act as proof of your expertise. These can include industry qualifications, special training, or a history of high performance. For example, a Fortinet or CrowdStrike certification shows that you are skilled in IT solutions. Mention these achievements when the time is right so that you reinforce your credibility.

Data also adds strength to your argument. In today's world, numbers are often very convincing. Share real facts about how you saved time or cut costs in past projects. You can even show charts or forecasts using tools like Power BI. This type of evidence shows you know your stuff and can align with your client's goals.

Finally, **experience** helps turn belief into trust. By sharing real-life stories—such as leading an important training programme or handling a big public sector contract—you prove that you understand the real challenges people face. Personal stories show that you have learned from hands-on situations, not just from theories.

Balancing empathy with authority is another crucial part of successful sales. Empathy means listening carefully to learn about the client's worries and needs. You can do this by asking thoughtful questions or summing up their points. For example, try saying, "It sounds like outdated systems are slowing down your team. Is that correct?" This shows you want to understand their problem.

Yet empathy alone will not close a deal. You also need to show confidence in your solutions. After you have shown you understand the problem, give a clear recommendation. Say something like, "Based on what you've told me, I suggest [specific solution] because it directly solves your challenges." This mix of kindness and strength helps you build trust while proving you can deliver results.

It is important to keep that balance. Be warm but also decisive and do not weaken your authority by apologising too much or offering vague advice. When you combine empathy and authority, people feel safe in trusting your ideas and they see you as a dependable guide.

Finally, integrity is a non-negotiable part of sales. You might be tempted to stretch the truth or over-promise for a quick win. However, people remember broken promises and once trust is lost, it can be very hard to get it back.

Being consistent shows that you are honest and reliable. Clients should always feel confident that you will do what you say. If your actions send mixed signals, they will start to doubt you. Since doubt can destroy a sale, it is vital to stay true to your word at all times. Doing so not only builds client loyalty but also boosts your own self-respect, which can help you stay strong even under pressure.

In the short term, cutting corners might look like an easy path to success, but it damages your reputation. In the long run, integrity sets you apart in a competitive market. A solid reputation as someone who does what they promise is a powerful advantage. By focusing on trust, empathy, authority and integrity, you create a firm base for long-term success and rewarding client relationships.

5. Mastering the First Contact: Setting the Tone

Making the Right First Impression in Sales

Have you ever felt judged the moment you walk into a room? In sales, these first few seconds matter more than many people realise. Psychologists call this the "primacy effect." It means that people form strong opinions based on the very first bits of information they receive. Research suggests that these opinions can take shape in just seven seconds.

Why does this matter? Because in sales, a shaky start can make your prospect doubt you, even if your pitch later improves. On the other hand, a confident and warm introduction can build trust straight away. Senior decision-makers, who often have limited time, are especially influenced by your initial behaviour. Make those first moments count.

Creating a Positive First Impression

To create a favourable impression, thorough preparation and genuine conduct are key. Before meeting a client, learn about their business needs, current obstacles and the solutions they might be seeking. Dress in a way that suits the situation but still feels comfortable and professional. Remember, non-verbal cues—like standing tall, giving a firm handshake and maintaining good eye contact—can speak louder than words.

Building a real connection is just as important. A bit of friendly conversation at the start can help everyone feel at ease. Try to be sincere and avoid scripted small talk. Listening with care also makes a difference. Nod to show you are following along, or briefly repeat what the other person said to confirm you have understood them correctly. This shows respect and helps form mutual trust.

But remember, you do not need to be perfect. Aim to show you are prepared, considerate and fully engaged from the moment you step into the room.

Structuring the Initial Conversation

When you speak with a new prospect, you have a great chance to build trust and learn what matters most to them. A simple framework helps you keep the conversation on track and productive. Here is how you can plan it:

- **Open with Rapport and Credibility**

Begin with a sincere comment about the person's business or industry. This breaks the ice. Then, briefly introduce yourself and your company. Include a short, clear value statement that links what you do to their possible challenges. For instance: "I help organisations like yours improve operations through tailored IT solutions."

- **Frame the Conversation**

Show respect for their time by stating what you would like to cover. For example: "I'd like to learn more about your main priorities, share how we've helped similar businesses and see if there is a good fit." This simple agenda keeps the discussion focused and efficient.

- **Ask Key Discovery Questions**

Next, encourage your prospect to share their goals and challenges. Ask open-ended questions like:
- "What are your top objectives for the coming year?"
- "What main obstacles keep you from reaching those goals?"
- "How do you usually evaluate solutions like ours?"
- "Have you worked with a similar provider before? What was that experience like?"

- **Practise Active Listening**

Show real interest in their responses. Summarise their points to check your understanding and ask follow-up questions to learn more. You might say, "Can you tell me more about that?" or "How does this affect your team's daily work?"

- **Summarise and Set Next Steps**

Finally, review the key points from your conversation and agree on what happens next. For instance, you could say: "It seems that improving efficiency and cutting costs are your main goals. Would you like to arrange a follow-up call or meeting to explore solutions?"

Following this simple plan helps you stay focused, learn valuable details about the prospect and set the stage for a successful relationship.

Mastering Your Introduction

A strong introduction should grab attention, establish trust and spark interest —all within just a few seconds. Here is a straightforward way to achieve that.

- **Step 1: Clarify Your Role**

Instead of only giving your job title, highlight how you can help. For example: "I specialise in helping organisations optimise their IT systems so they can scale smoothly."

- **Step 2: Establish Credibility**

People quickly judge how knowledgeable you are. Mention relevant experience or outcomes, but keep it short. For instance: "I've supported over 50 companies in this sector, helping them cut costs by up to 20%."

- **Step 3: Communicate Your Value Proposition**

Focus on outcomes that matter to them. Avoid empty claims and try to address their real needs. You could say: "We provide tailored solutions to solve your biggest challenges, making sure you see clear improvements in efficiency."

Practise your introduction until it flows naturally, but stay ready to adjust it if your prospect's questions or reactions lead you in a different direction.

Uncovering Buyer Priorities

Do you know your buyer's main concerns from the start? Finding out early on allows you to shape your pitch around what they truly need. To do this, you will want to ask open-ended questions and listen carefully.

Asking the Right Questions

Try to avoid simple "yes" or "no" prompts. Ask broader questions like:

- "What are you aiming to achieve in the next few months?"
- "Which issues are slowing down your progress at the moment?"
- "When thinking about a new solution, what factors carry the most weight?"

Practising Active Listening

Once they open up, really focus on their words. Show you are listening by nodding, paraphrasing their points and asking deeper questions. For instance, you might say: "It sounds like streamlining operations is your priority. Can you explain a bit more about what that involves?"

Before you wrap up, restate their key concerns or objectives. This confirms you have been paying attention and that you understand their situation.

Navigating Power Dynamics

In many sales conversations, you might meet people who have a lot of authority, such as top executives or skilled procurement specialists. Handling these power dynamics well can help you keep the upper hand. Here are a few tips:

- **Highlight Your Expertise**

Show that you know your field. Buyers respect deep knowledge, especially when it directly tackles their problems.

- **Ask Strategic Questions**

You can guide the conversation by asking meaningful, open-ended questions. This encourages the buyer to share more details about their pain points, which subtly gives you control.

- **Use Scarcity Wisely**

Let them see that your solution is unique. If you appear ready to walk away if necessary, you shift the balance of power in your favour.

- **Build Genuine Rapport**

Trust can reduce power imbalances. If you create a friendly atmosphere instead of a cold, purely business setting, people are less likely to use their authority aggressively.

Manage Expectations

Be clear about boundaries and goals from the beginning. This sets a professional tone and keeps the dialogue fair and balanced.

By applying these strategies, you can tackle challenging power dynamics with confidence. You will be more likely to form relationships that lead to positive outcomes for everyone involved.

6. The Power of Active Listening

In a competitive sales environment, success depends on understanding your customer's needs, problems and goals. This begins with a key skill: listening. But did you know there is a difference between simply hearing and truly listening? This difference can greatly improve how you sell.

Hearing is passive. You notice the sounds and words a customer uses, but you might not fully understand what they mean. In a sales conversation, this could lead to missed clues about feelings or concerns hiding beneath the words.

Listening, on the other hand, is active. It requires focus and genuine attention. You not only take in what is said but also respond in meaningful ways. By practising active listening, you pay close attention to the customer's tone, pauses, or repeated topics. These subtle signals can reveal deep worries or top priorities that they might not state outright.

When you listen carefully, you build trust. Customers who feel understood are more willing to share their thoughts and concerns. As a sales professional, this helps you move beyond standard sales scripts and instead offer custom solutions that solve each client's main problems. In a tough sales landscape, active listening is not just helpful—it is vital.

However, active listening goes beyond simply paying attention. It involves specific techniques that build better understanding and rapport. Three important methods include paraphrasing, summarising and reflective responses.

Paraphrasing

Paraphrasing means repeating what the customer has said in your own words. This helps confirm that you understand their message. For instance, if they say, "We are annoyed because our current provider often misses deadlines," you might reply, "So you need a provider that can deliver on time?" This shows you are listening and gives them a chance to correct you if needed.

Summarising

Summarising works well at the end of a conversation or after covering a main point. It involves recapping what has been discussed. For example, you might say, "To sum up, you want a system that works with your existing setup, is reliable and includes strong customer support." This confirms your understanding and invites the customer to clarify any details you might have missed.

Reflective Responses

Reflective responses show that you notice the emotions behind a customer's words. If they say they are frustrated, you could respond, "It seems this issue has caused a lot of stress for your team." This approach shows empathy and can deepen the relationship by making the customer feel truly heard.

In high-pressure sales roles, these methods can set you apart. By listening actively, you present yourself as a partner who focuses on solving the customer's problems.

Beyond spoken words, non-verbal signals are just as important. Hidden signs in both speech and body language can show what a buyer really wants or worries about.

Verbal Cues

Look for key words or phrases. If a customer says "I'm worried about…" it points to a concern. If they repeat words like "reliable" or "effective," it likely shows what matters most to them. Notice changes in tone too: excitement might mean agreement, while hesitation might mean doubt.

When you spot these signals, ask more questions. For example, if a customer says, "I just need this to work," you might ask, "What does 'work' mean for you? Do you mean it should be easy to use or dependable?" This gets them to share more details about what they truly want.

Non-Verbal Cues

Body language can reveal more than words. Leaning forward or looking directly at you often shows interest. Crossing arms or checking a watch can show they are uncomfortable or rushed. Even short facial expressions can indicate hidden worries. Silence also matters. If a buyer pauses before replying, they might be thinking carefully, so use open-ended questions to explore their thoughts.

Closing the Gap

Spotting these signals takes practice and empathy. As you speak with more customers and study their responses, your skills will grow stronger. By noticing hidden signs, you can tackle unspoken needs and form better connections.

Listening well is a main path to success in sales. It is more than taking in words; it is about understanding, showing empathy and answering in ways that build trust. When you pay attention, you show respect and can work together more effectively. This positions you as a trusted partner rather than just a salesperson.

Finally, good listening helps inside your own organisation too. When you value your team's ideas, you encourage creativity and better results. In both external and internal settings, listening is not just a skill—it is a smart strategy. By learning to listen effectively, you will uncover new possibilities, improve relationships and lay a strong base for lasting success.

7. Finding Common Ground: Aligning Objectives

Do you ever feel negotiation is a battle of opposing interests? It does not have to be. Instead of treating these conversations like a conflict, try focusing on shared objectives. When both you and your client aim for the same goals—like solving a pressing problem or finding a way to add value for everyone—instead of competing, you begin to work together. This shift in attitude makes the negotiation process smoother and also builds stronger relationships.

Shared goals help create trust. In sales, trust is the foundation of every successful discussion. When clients notice that you are genuinely interested in their success, they become more open and honest with you. By agreeing on outcomes that benefit both sides, your talks stop feeling like a standoff and start feeling like a partnership. This trust is especially important in high-stakes sales, where decisions are closely examined and strong bonds often decide the final outcome.

Focusing on what you have in common also simplifies the negotiation process. It cuts back on pointless posturing and encourages everyone to concentrate on real solutions. Making concessions feels more like an investment in the relationship than a loss. This attitude leads to a spirit of teamwork and, over time, supports long-lasting partnerships. By putting shared goals first, sales professionals not only close deals more effectively but also keep clients engaged and satisfied.

Techniques for Uncovering Shared Goals

Uncovering shared goals is easier when you use methods such as collaborative questioning and mutual problem-solving. These approaches allow salespeople to connect with clients on a deeper level and match interests more effectively.

Collaborative Questioning

Asking the right questions is vital in any negotiation. Collaborative questioning goes beyond basic needs and focuses on creating solutions together. You might begin with open-ended questions like, "What challenges are you facing at the moment?" or "What does success look like for you in this situation?" After learning about their main concerns, follow up with reflective questions, such as, "If we could address this specific challenge, how would it affect your targets?" These prompts show you care, build trust and set the stage for aligning your plan with their priorities.

Mutual Problem-Solving

Once you understand a client's challenges, move towards finding solutions together. Act like a partner, not just a salesperson. For example, if your client needs to reduce costs, you could explore ways to break the project into stages, saying, "What if we roll this out in phases so you can see results before expanding?" By working together on the solution, you create a sense of ownership. This lessens the chance of objections and helps strengthen the relationship.

These techniques demand genuine curiosity and a real drive to offer value. They lead to open conversations and turn negotiations into true partnerships, setting you up for success over the long term.

Building Rapport Through Mirroring

Mirroring is a subtle way to build a connection with a prospect. It involves copying certain behaviours, tone, or language they use. This tactic, known as the "chameleon effect," helps others feel understood and at ease. For example, if a client talks slowly and calmly, try matching their pace. If they lean forward in their chair, mirror that action in a natural way.

Mirroring includes both physical actions and language. If a client uses specific words—like "efficiency" or "speed"—try using those same words in your responses. This small step shows you are listening closely. However, stay genuine. If you mirror too much or too obviously, it may seem forced, which can damage trust. Use mirroring with subtlety and honesty for the best effect.

Balancing Buyer Needs with Sales Targets

Sales success means balancing your own goals with the buyer's needs. Think about forging a long-term connection rather than just making a one-time sale. Start by truly listening to the buyer's requirements. Ask questions that show empathy and gather details about their pain points. Once you have a clear idea of what they want, explain how your solution matches their goals while still meeting your sales targets.

Honesty is crucial. If there are any limits to what you can offer, be open about them. This honesty builds respect and avoids problems later. Make sure any discounts or alterations still fit your broader strategy. After finalising the deal, continue to check in on the client's progress. This shows commitment, builds trust and paves the way for future opportunities.

Turning Alignment into Agreement

Once you have aligned with a prospect, how do you turn that shared vision into an actual agreement? Start by making it clear that you are on the same page. You might say, "It sounds like we agree this solution covers your main needs—am I right?" Getting that confirmation sets the stage for the next step.

Then, move towards concrete actions. Rather than asking, "What do you think?", try asking, "What would you need from me to move forward?" This encourages the prospect to see the solution as the logical next step. Tie their commitment to the goals they have already shared. For instance, "Putting this plan in place by the end of next quarter will help you reach your efficiency goals. Does that timeline work for you?"

Be ready to address objections early and make the next steps simple. When people feel informed and reassured, they are more likely to say yes. By guiding the discussion towards a mutual agreement, you do more than just close deals. You also build a lasting partnership built on trust.

Remember, true success in sales is not about winning every negotiation at any cost. It is about forming lasting partnerships that serve everyone's best interests. By concentrating on shared goals, building trust and guiding conversations towards workable agreements, you can thrive in even the toughest sales environments and secure impressive results.

8. Overcoming Objections: Turning 'No' into 'Yes'

It is important to know why buyers say "no" or hesitate. Have you ever wondered if they simply do not understand the benefits, or if the price feels too high? By learning the main reasons behind their objections, you can respond with confidence and move closer to making a sale.

Common Buyer Objections and Strategies to Address Them

- **Price Concerns**

Price is one of the most frequent objections. Some buyers may feel the cost is too high compared to the value they expect. Others might not see how your solution will help them save money or gain an advantage.

How to Address Price Concerns:

- **Show Clear Value**: Explain exactly how your solution meets the buyer's goals. Focus on the unique advantages that make the price worth it.

- **Use Data and Stories**: Share stories or facts that prove how customers have seen a good return on investment (ROI). This helps buyers see why the cost is justified.

- **Reframe the Conversation:** You might say, "I understand budget is a concern. Many of our clients once felt the same, but they discovered the long-term benefits easily covered the initial expense. Let me share an example."

- **Timing Issues**

Sometimes, buyers delay decisions because of other tasks, slow approval processes, or a fear of moving too quickly. These concerns often show that the buyer is unsure, not that they are rejecting you.

How to Address Timing Issues:

- **Highlight the Cost of Waiting:** Help buyers see the risks or lost opportunities of putting things off.

- **Create a Sense of Urgency:** Show how your solution can help right now and in the future.

- **Work Together:** You could say, "I understand timing matters. Shall we discuss how to fit this into your current plans?"

- **Trust and Compatibility Concerns**

Some buyers hesitate because they do not fully trust the salesperson or worry about how well the solution will work for them. This might be due to past bad experiences or not having enough proof that your offer is reliable.

How to Address Trust and Compatibility Concerns:

- **Build Rapport:** Spend time creating a strong relationship with open, honest communication.

- **Offer Evidence:** Provide demonstrations, success stories, or references from happy customers.

- **Ask Open Questions:** For example, "What concerns do you have about how this might work for your organisation?"

Turning Objections into Opportunities

• **Acknowledge and Pivot**

When a buyer objects, it is best to admit their concern right away without being defensive. This shows respect and creates a good setting for problem-solving. For instance, if someone says, "Your solution is too expensive," reply, "I understand budget is a big factor for many organisations." This shows empathy and understanding.

Then, guide the conversation towards value. You might add, "While cost is important, many of our clients found that the savings and efficiency they gained were well worth the investment."

• **Seek Clarity**

Sometimes, an objection hides a deeper problem. Try asking, "Could you tell me more about what is causing this concern?" This may reveal the real issue, helping you solve it properly.

• **Use Storytelling**

Sharing success stories can turn ideas into real, relatable outcomes. For example, "One of our clients felt the same way, but after using our solution, they achieved [specific result] and saw how it made a real difference."

- **Confirm and Close**

Once you address an objection, check that the buyer is satisfied. This helps clear up any confusion and allows you to move forward. For instance, you can ask, "Does that solve your worry?" If they say yes, bring the conversation back to the main topic and focus on taking the next steps to close the deal.

Objections are normal in sales. They often show a buyer's worries or risk concerns, but they also open a door for you to show your skill and earn their trust. By listening, showing empathy and keeping the focus on value, you can turn many objections into moments of genuine connection. This is the key difference that sets top salespeople apart from the rest.

9. Creating Value: Shifting the Focus from Price to Benefits

Have you ever wondered why price stands out so much when you're choosing a product or service? For many buyers, it feels like the clearest factor to compare. In competitive markets or when budgets are tight, buyers must show they are spending money wisely. They need to prove value, compare options and manage costs. As a result, price is often the easiest way to measure these things.

A lower price can also appear less risky. After all, if you pay less, it might seem you have more room to avoid a costly mistake. This way of thinking is common when buyers do not fully understand a product's features. If sellers fail to show how their solution provides real value, then price becomes the most important deciding factor.

Cost is about more than just money. Buyers might worry about their reputation at work if they choose an expensive solution that fails. They might feel it is safer to pick the cheaper option, even if it is not the best in quality. When people do not see the bigger picture of value, the safest bet is often the cheaper one.

Shifting the Focus from Price to Value

How can sales professionals help buyers see beyond the price tag? First, they should accept that cost is a real concern. Rather than ignoring it, they can turn the conversation towards value. By discussing long-term benefits, time-saving features and strategic gains, they can show buyers what they stand to gain, rather than just what they pay.

It is important to explain both visible and hidden benefits. These benefits speak to different parts of a buyer's decision. When sellers can clearly share these points, they stand out from the competition.

Tangible Benefits: The Measurable Impact

Tangible benefits are easy to measure, such as lower costs, higher income, or faster processes. For example, if a piece of software saves 10 hours of manual work each week, a company can quickly see how much money those hours are worth.

Be specific when you talk about these benefits. Use real numbers or stories that show results. Phrases like "Our solution cuts costs by 25% in three months" are very convincing. Facts and figures build trust and help buyers see clear proof.

Intangible Benefits: The Emotional Connection

Have you ever felt relief when a purchase gives you peace of mind? This feeling is what we call an intangible benefit. It is harder to measure, but it can be just as powerful. Think about a cybersecurity solution. It might not only block threats, but it also gives the buyer confidence and reassurance.

Sharing these kinds of benefits requires good storytelling. Describe real-life examples or vivid scenarios. Help the buyer imagine their worries disappearing as they use the product or service. For instance, say, "You'll feel at ease knowing your business is protected from online threats." This emotional angle can often seal the deal.

Tailoring Your Approach

Different audiences care about different things. Senior managers or directors might focus on return on investment (ROI), while end-users might want an easier tool to use each day. Combine data and storytelling for a balanced message. You could say, "Our client saw a 30% boost in productivity and also reported their team felt less stressed."

Active listening is also vital. Ask questions, learn about your buyer's biggest problems and then show how your solution answers those needs. By mixing both tangible and intangible benefits, you build a strong case that meets logical and emotional needs.

The Power of Storytelling

In a crowded market, storytelling can help you stand out. It adds a human touch to your pitch, taps into emotions and helps buyers remember you.

Using Anecdotes

Short, personal stories make your presentation more interesting. Rather than simply saying your product lowers downtime by 30%, tell a story about a small factory that avoided a major outage thanks to your solution. Show the initial panic they felt and the relief when your product did its job. Real-life details bring your results to life.

Leveraging Case Studies

Case studies are like detailed stories. Walk the buyer through another customer's journey, from the issues they faced to the solution you provided. Back your claims with facts, such as how much time, money, or effort was saved. Relate this to the buyer's own situation so they can imagine the same success happening for them.

Making It Relevant

Always tailor your stories to your current buyer. If they can see themselves in your examples, your pitch becomes more than just information—it becomes an inspiring vision. Rather than listing features, show them a story they can believe in.

Quantifying Value Through ROI

Return on Investment (ROI) can be a strong tool for proving financial value. It cuts through confusion and provides a clear number. Decision-makers often want hard figures, so ROI is a simple way to satisfy that need.

Calculating ROI

ROI is calculated using a basic formula:

$$\text{ROI} = \left(\frac{\text{Net Profit}}{\text{Investment Cost}}\right) \times 100\%$$

For example, if someone spends £50,000 on your service and gains £150,000 in return, their ROI would be:

$$\text{ROI} = \left(\frac{50{,}000}{150{,}000 - 50{,}000}\right) \times 100 = 200\,\%$$

A 200% ROI is quite eye-catching and gives strong proof of value.

Expanding ROI Metrics

There are other ways to show the value of your product:

- **Payback Period**: How long before the buyer recovers the initial cost?

$$\text{Payback Period} = \frac{\text{Investment Cost}}{\text{Annual Net Savings}}$$

- **Lifetime Value:** The full benefit your solution gives over its entire life cycle.

- **Opportunity Cost:** What does the buyer miss out on by not choosing your product?

Presenting ROI Effectively

Use visuals like charts or graphs to make ROI data easy to understand. A finance director may want all the numbers, while an operations manager might be more interested in how much time is saved. Always shape your presentation to match the audience.

Shifting Focus to Total Cost of Ownership (TCO)

Many people only focus on the first cost they see, but the Total Cost of Ownership (TCO) includes all expenses from purchase to replacement. When you share TCO, you encourage buyers to think about long-term value, not just the upfront price.

A product that costs more at the start might save money in the future if it lasts longer or needs fewer repairs. Give concrete examples and data to show how a cheaper choice might lead to bigger costs later. Ask questions like, "How much does lost time cost your team?" or "What is the long-term impact of replacing equipment every two years?"

Becoming a Trusted Adviser

Aim to be more than just a salesperson. Show genuine interest in your buyer's success. Tailor your advice to their unique needs. By honestly focusing on TCO, you address cost worries and show that you want to help them make the best decision.

In the end, when you stand by the buyer's goals and show them a path to better outcomes, you earn trust. As a result, price becomes just one factor in a larger conversation about true value.

10. The Power of Silence: Using Pauses to Your Advantage

Silence is often overlooked in sales. Yet, when used wisely, it can shift the mood of a conversation, create a sense of pressure and guide buying decisions. Many salespeople find silence uncomfortable and rush to fill it. But if you learn to pause and let silence do some of the talking, you can make your sales conversations far more powerful.

The Psychology of Silence

Silence can feel awkward for most people. Have you ever noticed how a few quiet seconds can make someone eager to speak? When you ask a question and then pause, the other person usually feels the need to break the silence. Often, they will share useful details about their preferences or worries. This information helps you tailor your sales approach to their real needs.

In negotiations, silence also proves your confidence. If a client objects or makes a counter-offer, remaining silent can make them reconsider. It shows you believe in your offer and are taking their concerns seriously. In turn, they may be more willing to reach a better agreement. Silence can also show thoughtfulness. This builds trust because it shows you truly value their perspective.

Breaking Expectations

Most buyers think salespeople will do most of the talking. Pausing at key moments can surprise them and draw them in. When you speak less, the focus naturally shifts to the buyer. This encourages them to share more, creating a conversation that is both deeper and more balanced. By doing this, you stand out from salespeople who only push their own agenda. Your thoughtful approach shows that you listen and care.

Strategic Uses of Silence

Knowing how and when to use silence in sales can be a real game-changer. Here are some moments when a well-placed pause can make all the difference:

- **After Presenting an Offer**
Once you present your proposal or price, resist the urge to explain further. Give the buyer time to process. Their first reaction often reveals important clues about their concerns or priorities.

- **Following a Concession**
If you decide to offer a concession, stay quiet afterwards. This may prevent the buyer from pushing for even more. It can also encourage them to meet you halfway or move forward in the conversation.

- **When Addressing Objections**
After acknowledging an objection, pause. You might be surprised at how often the buyer will add more details or offer a solution themselves. This reduces the need for you to defend your position.

- **After Asking for Commitment**

Questions like "Would you like to move forward?" should be followed by silence. This gives the buyer a moment to think and increases the chance of a "yes."

- **In High-Tension Moments**

Emotions can run high when discussing money or deadlines. Silence allows everyone to cool down and gather their thoughts. It shows you are listening and can help ease stress in the room.

Building Confidence in Silence

Staying quiet can be harder than it looks. Here are some tips to help you master this skill:

- **Count to Five**: After you ask a question or make a point, silently count to five before speaking again. It might feel odd at first, but it encourages the buyer to respond.
- **Active Listening**: Focus on their words, tone and body language. When you listen closely, you become less tempted to fill every gap in the conversation.
- **Role-Playing:** Practise with a friend or colleague. Insert pauses on purpose and see how it affects their responses. This builds your confidence in using silence.
- **Mindfulness Exercises**: Spend a few minutes each day meditating or breathing deeply. Becoming comfortable with stillness will help you resist the urge to speak too soon.
- **Reflective Journaling:** After each sales call, note any moments when you felt a need to fill the silence. Analyse why you felt that way and how you might handle it better next time.

Less is More

Remember, your sales conversation needs balance. Too much talking can drown out your message and leave the buyer overwhelmed. Confidence grows when you know your product well enough to sum it up simply. Trust your expertise and trust the process.

Silence is not the same as doing nothing. In fact, it is a powerful tool that shows confidence, builds trust and guides better decisions. Speak wisely, listen carefully and embrace those silent moments. When used at the right time, silence becomes far more than a pause—it becomes a statement.

11. Reading the Room: Body Language and Non-Verbal Cues

Have you ever noticed how someone's posture or a simple hand gesture can influence the mood of a conversation? Body language is a silent yet powerful tool in any negotiation, especially in high-pressure sales. Before a single agreement is signed, non-verbal cues can shape how people perceive you and your message.

Posture and Confidence
Your posture often gives the first clue about your confidence. Standing up straight with your feet on the ground and your shoulders back shows self-assuredness. By contrast, slouching or fidgeting can suggest worry or boredom. When you lean forward slightly, it signals interest, but leaning in too much can feel invasive. Aim for a balanced stance that shows you are calm but also engaged.

Gestures and Clarity
Simple hand movements can add impact to what you say. Open palms usually mean honesty and openness, while folded arms or pointing fingers

may look hostile or defensive. Avoid waving your hands too wildly, as it can be off-putting or distracting. A gentle, controlled gesture helps highlight key points and builds trust.

Facial Expressions and Eye Contact
Facial expressions can either create connection or break it. A genuine smile usually sets a warm tone, but overdoing it might appear fake. Meanwhile, eye contact sends a message of respect and honesty. Look at the other person steadily but naturally. Glancing away now and then can show you are thinking, but avoiding eye contact too often may suggest lack of confidence or interest.

In fast-paced sales, it is not only vital to be aware of your own body language but also to observe the other person's non-verbal cues. Do they mirror your gestures? Are they leaning away or looking elsewhere? These small signs can reveal more about their thoughts and feelings than you might expect.

Mastering basic body language skills can transform negotiations from tense struggles into calmer, more productive conversations. When you use posture, gestures and facial expressions to your advantage, you gain an edge in tough situations.

Reading Buyer Signals

Strong negotiators also recognise the value of interpreting a buyer's non-verbal signals. By spotting interest and disinterest early, you can adapt your approach and build a stronger connection.

Recognising Signs of Interest

Watch for open postures such as uncrossed arms or legs. A slight lean forward or a few nods usually means the buyer is listening carefully. Regular eye contact is also a good sign that they are interested in what you are saying.

Positive words can reveal interest, too. Phrases like, "That makes sense," or "Could you tell me more?" show they are picturing how your product or service fits into their needs. If they start taking notes, it is another signal that they want more detail.

Spotting Disinterest

On the other hand, crossed arms or legs often signal discomfort or a guarded mindset. If the buyer leans back or turns away, they may be trying to create distance. Constantly checking a phone or clock suggests they are not fully present in the conversation.

Short replies or a complete lack of questions are also warning signs. Statements like, "We'll think about it" or "I'm not sure this is right for us" might be polite ways of showing hesitancy. Recognising these signals means you can adjust your pitch.

Adapting to Signals

When you notice signs of interest, encourage the buyer to share more. Ask questions that help them connect your offering to their specific needs. If you sense disinterest, address it directly. Find out what might be holding them back and reframe your value proposition so it speaks to their concerns.

By paying attention to these signals, you can shift your approach in real time. This skill could turn a potential rejection into a fresh opportunity.

Non-Verbal Cues That Speak Louder Than Words

In a busy, high-pressure sales environment, what you do not say can be just as important as what you do. Body language, facial expressions and even moments of silence can reveal how a buyer truly feels. The best salespeople watch for these clues and adapt their style on the spot.

For Example
If a buyer leans back with crossed arms, they might be unsure or doubtful. Instead of pushing ahead with more details, pause and ask, "How do you feel about what we've covered so far?" This question invites them to share worries so you can address them.

Micro Expressions

Tiny changes in someone's face can also tell you a lot. An eyebrow lifted in surprise or a slight frown can suggest shock, confusion, or even discomfort. If this happens during a pricing discussion, it might indicate the price is higher than expected. In that moment, you can stress the benefits of your solution or offer a relevant case study to calm their concerns.

Embracing Silence

Sometimes a person goes quiet because they are thinking. Do not rush in to fill the silence. By waiting patiently, you give them room to process your points. After a short pause, you might say, "What are your thoughts right now?" to learn more about their perspective.

Paying close attention to all of these non-verbal signals can help you tailor your pitch more effectively. When you use emotional intelligence in this way, you will find more opportunities to close deals.

The Power of Eye Contact and Gestures

In a world where first impressions count, eye contact and gestures work together to make you look trustworthy and confident. But how do you master these subtle acts?

Eye Contact

Steady eye contact shows you are honest and interested in what the other person has to say. Yet too much eye contact can be intimidating. Aim for a natural pattern: look at the buyer when you make an important point, then briefly glance away when thinking. This rhythm makes you appear calm and thoughtful.

Gestures

Using your hands to highlight key ideas helps people understand what you are saying. When you talk about a feature or benefit, a small forward movement of the hand can emphasise it. Crossing your arms or fidgeting, however, can send the wrong signal. Think of gestures as a way to underline your words, not overshadow them.

Combining careful eye contact and purposeful gestures can create a lasting impression. You appear composed, clear and genuine. This is exactly what customers look for in a trusted partner. In a crowded market, these small actions often make a big difference.

Cultural Awareness in Body Language

One thing many people overlook is how culture influences body language. If you sell to clients around the world, be mindful that the same gesture can mean very different things in different places.

Eye Contact Differences

In many Western cultures, making direct eye contact suggests confidence. In some Asian cultures, however, prolonged eye contact might seem impolite or aggressive. For instance, in Japan, modesty is valued, so looking someone in the eye for too long may come across as rude.

Gestures Around the Globe

The thumbs-up gesture, popular in Western regions to show approval, could be disrespectful in some parts of the Middle East. The "OK" hand sign, where the thumb and forefinger form a circle, might mean "zero" in France and can be considered offensive in Brazil.

Posture and Personal Space

In Latin America, people often stand closer during conversations. This closeness is a sign of warmth. Meanwhile, Northern Europeans usually prefer more personal space and moving too near might make them uneasy.

Shaking Hands

Even handshakes are not the same everywhere. In Germany, a strong handshake is seen as professional. In India, you might offer a softer handshake and nod your head. Understanding these differences helps you avoid making anyone uncomfortable.

Facial Expressions

A friendly smile is usually good, but some cultures reserve smiles for close friends or family. In Russia, for example, constant smiling may be seen as suspicious or insincere.

For sales professionals, preparation and observation are key. When you learn about your client's cultural background—and watch how they behave in person—you can match your own body language to what is most appropriate. This shows respect and helps you build trust faster.

Body language is a powerful part of communication that many overlook, especially in cross-cultural and competitive sales situations. By using the right posture, gestures and facial expressions, you can build stronger connections and close more deals. At the same time, paying attention to cultural differences shows your clients that you respect their customs and way of doing business.

After all, truly successful sales hinge not just on the words we use, but on the messages we send without speaking. Are you ready to use body language to your advantage?

12. Anchoring and Counter-Offers: The Numbers Game

Have you ever noticed how the first number in a conversation can change the entire mood? This idea is called anchoring. Anchoring is a strategy used in both psychology and negotiation. It sets a reference point—often the first offer—that shapes all the other figures discussed later on.

Why does anchoring matter so much? As soon as someone mentions an opening price, people start seeing that figure as a fair range. If you give a high first price, others may see your product or service as more valuable right away. But if you do not anchor first, someone else may grab control and steer the deal in their favour.

Shaping Expectations

When you place an anchor, you guide how the other person thinks about the deal. The first number works like a benchmark. All offers that follow seem close to that point. Because of this, it is wise to pick your anchor carefully. You might go higher to allow room for a discount later. Or you might choose a smaller but more precise number to show your best terms. Always consider the other side's reaction before you make your move.

Possible Pitfalls

Of course, anchoring does not always work perfectly. If your opening figure feels rude or out of touch, you can lose the deal. Skilled negotiators seek a balance between being bold and staying believable. A good anchor sets a strong tone but also keeps the door open for further discussion.

How to Set an Effective Anchor

- **Do Your Research**

It is important to know your market and the other person's needs. If your service usually sells for £8,000, you might start at £10,000 to give yourself some bargaining room.

- **Aim High but Stay Fair**

People often want to meet in the middle. A slightly higher first offer can make your final price more attractive, as long as it does not seem unreasonable.

- **Manage the Timing**

Set your anchor once you have shown why your product or service is special. When buyers see how you solve their problems, they become more willing to accept your price.

- **Give Proof and Reasons**

Show facts or industry data to back up your anchor. For example, you might say, "Our service costs £10,000 because it can cut your running costs by 20%." This shows real value, not just a random figure.

- **Prepare for Pushback**

Even with a strong anchor, expect the other side to argue. Remain calm and keep pointing out the strengths of your offer. If you can, add a sweetener—

like flexible payment terms—to show good faith and keep the conversation on track.

Facing a Buyer's Anchor

Buyers often try to anchor low. Do you have to accept their first number? Not at all. If they throw out a very low price, stay cool. Getting upset might harm trust.

Instead, turn the talk back to the value you offer. You could say, "That's an interesting start. Let's think about how our service benefits your organisation." This way, you shift the spotlight to your strengths, not just the cost.

Then, respond with clear evidence and success stories. You might say, "I understand your position, but our fees match the industry standards and the results we deliver." Keep your voice respectful and friendly. Show that you want a fair agreement for both sides. If they still will not budge, a brief pause can sometimes encourage them to review their stance.

Timing Your Counter-Offer

The moment you choose to counter is as important as what you say. If you reply too soon, you may seem hurried. Wait until the buyer fully states their position. Then pause and think. This pause shows you take their offer seriously.

When you do answer, try to stay positive. Instead of saying, "I can't do that," say, "I have a different idea that might benefit us both." This approach keeps things friendly and keeps the deal moving forward.

If you are in a tight spot, you might try a conditional counter-offer. For example, "If you agree to a two-year contract, I can lower the price." This allows for compromise without giving too much away all at once.

Anchors in Competitive Sales

In busy sales settings, a strong anchor can mean the difference between winning a deal or losing out. People often stick to the first number they hear. This is why you should anchor with confidence and solid research behind you.

If the buyer attempts to anchor first, do not simply go along with it. Present your own figure and explain why it is fair. Remind the buyer of the benefits they receive from your offer. Above all, stay calm and flexible. By using the right anchor at the right time, you can guide the conversation, uphold your worth and build stronger business relationships.

13. Navigating Deadlocks: Staying Calm Under Pressure

Have you ever felt stuck in a conversation with a potential client? A deadlock happens when you and the other person cannot move forward. This often occurs in high-stakes sales, where both sides may feel cautious about giving in. If your talks keep repeating the same points, or if your once-enthusiastic prospect becomes hesitant or defensive, you may be facing a deadlock. Another clue is when deadlines keep getting pushed back without good reason.

Pay attention to what people say and how they say it. Phrases like, "We're not certain," or "We need more time," might seem harmless, but they can hide deeper worries. Notice nonverbal signs too, such as long pauses or a lack of energy. These can reveal serious resistance. Remember that a deadlock often involves big issues, like conflicting goals or a breakdown in trust, which go beyond simple buyer indecision.

Early recognition of these warning signs helps you respond more quickly. You can refocus on the customer's main problems, adjust your product's value statement, or bring higher-level decision-makers into the discussion.

Spotting a deadlock is not about giving up. Instead, it's about taking a step back, resetting the tone and seizing a chance to build a better path forward.

Breaking Through an Impasse

Deadlocks usually arise when people stick firmly to their positions or do not trust each other's solutions. To move past this, you can use different methods that bring both sides closer to a win-win outcome.

Reframing the Conversation

Sometimes, you need to shift how you present the problem. For example, if your customer is only focused on cost, try talking about value instead. Show how your product solves their unique concerns or offers lasting benefits. You can also ask open-ended questions like, "What would success look like for you?" or "Could we talk about the main goals for this project?" These questions can uncover shared interests and steer the conversation towards cooperation.

Finding Areas of Compromise

Do you think compromise means surrender? It does not have to. True compromise involves finding solutions that satisfy both sides. You can suggest changes to delivery dates, bundle extra services, or adjust contract details. If the client worries about cost, perhaps offer more flexible payment plans or a small discount on add-ons. Showing you can bend on certain points often lowers tension and helps everyone feel heard.

Involving Third Parties

When negotiations stall, a neutral party can offer fresh ideas. This might be a specialist within your company who understands complex technical issues. It could also be an outside mediator trained in conflict resolution. Such individuals can see the problem from a distance, suggest new approaches and help both sides save face. Their neutral stance allows them to offer solutions neither party had thought of before.

Maintaining a Cooperative Tone

Throughout this process, keep your tone helpful rather than combative. Show genuine respect for the other person's worries and explain that you want a fair outcome for all. Building trust is essential if you want to break deadlocks and a warm, understanding approach is usually more powerful than a hard push. When trust grows, difficult talks become opportunities to strengthen relationships instead of tearing them down.

The Power of Patience

In the high-pressure world of sales, it's easy to feel like you must rush every deal. But have you ever noticed how patience can make all the difference? When you face a deadlock, you may feel tempted to force a solution or offer big concessions too soon. Instead, try taking a breath and letting the conversation develop. By staying calm, you can learn more about the client's hidden needs or concerns. Silence can also work in your favour, as it often prompts the other person to speak more freely.

Patience is not weakness; it shows confidence. It signals that you are steady, in control and genuinely interested in understanding the other side. This approach lowers tension and may lead to creative answers that neither side thought of at first. It also helps you avoid rushing into decisions that might harm the partnership later.

Bringing in Outside Perspectives

Sometimes, even your patience and good strategies are not enough. When trust has worn thin or issues seem impossible to fix, an outside perspective can help. A mediator, trusted colleague, or consultant can bridge gaps in communication. They might also explain difficult topics in a clearer way.

Know when it's the right time to bring in help. If you do it too early, your partners might think you lack confidence. But if you wait too long, the conflict might grow worse. Choose someone who is truly neutral and has the knowledge to address the problem. Make sure everyone agrees on this person's role from the start. This openness shows you want to find a fair answer.

Taking Time to Regroup

In the rush to close deals, it is easy to keep pushing forward without stopping. Yet, taking a short break can give you a fresh point of view. You can look at what is working, what is not and decide if you need to change course. This pause not only helps you think strategically but also lowers stress. Sales can be intense and burnout can cost you important deals.

Stepping back for a moment can also create a chance to talk with teammates. They might offer new ideas or point out gaps you have missed. By sharing your challenges, you often find solutions that seem obvious once someone else suggests them. These breaks do not slow you down in the long run. Instead, they help you refocus so you can move forward with a better plan.

In the end, breaking deadlocks and building strong sales relationships is a continuous process. By spotting warning signs early, using fresh ideas and staying patient, you can turn even the toughest standoffs into opportunities.

A little flexibility and understanding often lead to wins for both sides—and that is what successful sales is all about.

14. Negotiating in Competitive Situations: Outmanoeuvring Rivals

In fiercely competitive environments, knowing who you are up against can make all the difference. Have you ever wondered how your competitors plan their next move or why they attract certain customers? By studying their strategies, you will see where your own product or service can shine.

Begin by identifying your main competitors. These include direct rivals who offer the same type of solution, as well as indirect competitors who solve the same problem in different ways. Make a list of at least five primary competitors and note their position in the market.

Next, look closely at what they do well and where they fall short. Examine their website, social media pages, customer reviews and press releases. You might spot clues in their marketing messages, pricing, or product features. For example, a competitor with strong online advertising might have poor customer service. This could be your chance to highlight your reliability and attention to detail.

Tools like LinkedIn Sales Navigator let you see who works at rival companies and who their clients might be. SEMrush or Ahrefs help you learn about their web traffic and keywords, while review platforms such as Trustpilot and G2 reveal what customers really think.

It is also a good idea to compare your own performance with theirs. Look at pricing, how many new customers you both attract and your share of the market. Talk to prospects and current clients to gather informal feedback on how they view each competitor's value.

Always focus on insights you can use. Listing a competitor's strengths alone does not help much, so think about how you can surpass them. For instance, if a competitor is known for speed but is not flexible, you could promote your ability to be both quick and adaptable.

Finally, keep your finger on the pulse of change. Markets shift fast and fresh information helps you update your approach. By staying informed, you can respond to new threats and remain ahead of the competition.

Identifying Buyer Alternatives

When speaking to potential buyers, it is important to know what other options they are considering. Buyers often compare your offer to many different solutions before making a decision. If you understand these choices, you can adjust your message and stand out.

Begin by asking open-ended questions. For example, "What other solutions have you explored?" or "How does this compare to the other options on your list?" These questions give buyers the freedom to share what they really think. Listen carefully to their tone of voice and any hesitation. You might learn which features or benefits they value the most.

Meanwhile, do some research on your buyer's industry to see which rivals they might be looking at. If you are pitching cloud security software to an IT director, you should know who the leading providers are. This extra homework can help you anticipate objections and show why your product or service is different.

Once you know the buyer's alternatives, use that knowledge in your discussions. Focus on the features or benefits that matter most to them. For example, if they say another supplier is cheaper but offers poor support, you can emphasise your reliable customer service.

You might also ask, "If you could change one thing about the other solutions, what would it be?" Their answer tells you exactly where competitors fall short. This is your chance to highlight how you can fill that gap.

By exploring a buyer's alternatives, you take control of the sales conversation. You show that you are not just selling a product but helping them solve a problem in the best possible way. This builds trust and can lead to stronger relationships.

Differentiating Beyond Price

In the hard-hitting world of sales, it is easy to lower your price to win a deal. Yet many experienced salespeople warn that battling on price alone often leads to smaller profits and weaker value. How can you avoid this race to the bottom?

Instead of focusing on cost, highlight what makes your product or service truly unique. These Unique Selling Points (USPs) might include excellent customer service, fresh ideas, or dependable results. Here are four ways to stand out:

- **Lead with Excellent Service**

We are living in an age where customer experience matters more than ever. Make sure your service is outstanding by personalising your approach and staying in touch even after the sale. Regular check-ins can strengthen loyalty and uncover new business opportunities.

- **Innovate Constantly**

Innovation does not just mean adding new features. It can also mean offering flexible payment terms, using technology to speed up processes, or sharing training resources with customers. If you can present creative solutions, you will keep your clients interested and engaged.

- **Be Unfailingly Reliable**

Reliability builds trust. Meet every deadline, keep your promises and stand by your customers when they need you most. Your reputation for being dependable will set you apart from rivals who compete only on price.

- **Demonstrate Tangible Value**

Show customers exactly what they gain by choosing you. Use case studies, testimonials, or data to prove the long-term benefits of your product or service. Help buyers see how you can improve their efficiency, reduce risks, or boost customer satisfaction.

When you focus on your value rather than the price, you tell a more powerful story. Strong USPs can make you a trusted adviser, not just another vendor. This approach may take more effort, but it can lead to better results and long-lasting business relationships.

Using Scarcity And Urgency

Emotions often guide our decisions, especially in sales. Have you noticed how limited-time offers make people act faster? Scarcity and urgency play into our fear of missing out and can help motivate buyers to sign on the dotted line.

Scarcity works by showing that something is limited or exclusive. It might be a low stock count or a special deal that will not last. For example, telling a prospect "We only have a few units left at this price" can move them to action. However, you must always tell the truth. Pretending there is a limited offer when there is not will damage trust in the long run.

Urgency focuses on time limits. Reminders like "This deal ends on Friday" or "Prices go up next month" prompt buyers to make decisions sooner. People dislike missing out on a good offer, so they will prioritise your deal to avoid losing out.

Of course, scarcity and urgency work best when combined with genuine value. Without real benefits, these tactics can feel pushy or false. Buyers want to see how your solution solves their problem, saves them money, or improves their workflow. If you can prove value and add urgency, you create a powerful reason to close the deal.

Managing Multiple Stakeholders

In some sales situations, you may face several stakeholders with different goals or concerns. Each person has a voice in the final decision, which can make things complicated. So, how can you steer the deal in your favour without causing conflict?

- **Map the Stakeholders**

First, find out who is involved. Is there a key decision-maker who holds the purse strings? Are there influencers who can sway others? Write down these roles and how much power each person has in the company.

- **Build One-on-One Connections**

Speak individually to each stakeholder whenever possible. This private setting can encourage them to share problems, fears, or goals they might not voice in front of the group. Use what you learn to show how your solution benefits everyone.

- **Use Data for Alignment**

Facts and figures can bring people together. Show how your product or service solves a common issue. Highlight strong returns on investment or solid cost savings, so stakeholders see that your solution makes sense for the entire group.

- **Resolve Conflicts Early**

Disagreements between stakeholders are normal. Do not ignore them. Instead, ask open-ended questions to learn more about each side's main worries. Then, suggest compromises that meet the most important needs. If you act as a fair guide, you can earn their trust and keep the discussion on track.

- **Aim for Group Agreement**

Do not push for a final decision until everyone agrees on the main points. Summarise any agreements reached in each meeting to check you are all on the same page. Moving too fast can annoy key players and put the sale at risk.

Managing multiple stakeholders requires patience, clear communication and a willingness to listen. If you can guide different people towards a common goal, they will not only accept your proposal but may also see you as a reliable partner.

By using these strategies—understanding competitors, identifying buyer alternatives, showing true value, applying scarcity and urgency properly and uniting stakeholders—you stand a better chance of thriving in today's tough sales landscape. Think of each of these steps as part of a bigger plan to help your customers and to set your own solution apart from the crowd.

15. Closing the Deal: Timing and Tactics

Have you ever wondered why some salespeople seem to know the perfect moment to close a deal? Recognising buying signals is often the key. These signals show when a potential buyer is ready to take the next step, allowing you to seal the deal with confidence.

- **Verbal Buying Signals**

Verbal signals are the clearest indicators. Pay close attention to any questions about timing, price, or contract details. For example, if someone asks, "How soon can we start?" they are probably imagining themselves using your product or service. Statements like, "This could really help us," also suggest they are ready to move forward. Even offhand remarks such as, "We've been looking for something like this," point to a shift in their mindset.

- **Non-Verbal Buying Signals**

Non-verbal cues are just as important as what people say. Positive body language, like leaning in, nodding, or keeping steady eye contact, often shows strong interest. A relaxed posture can mean the person feels at ease with your proposal. If they start taking notes, it shows they are thinking more seriously. Also, notice if objections suddenly stop. That might mean the buyer has no more worries and is prepared to move ahead.

- **Closing the Deal**

When you notice these signals, it is time to act. You could say, "It sounds like you are ready to move forward. Shall we finalise the details?" Avoid loading the conversation with extra details at this point. Instead, summarise the main benefits and outline the next steps. Recognising and using buying signals can turn a missed chance into a signed contract.

Structuring a Compelling Offer

Selling in a competitive world is not just about pushing products. You must create offers that match the buyer's top priorities while meeting your own sales goals. How can you strike this perfect balance?

- **Understand Buyer Priorities**

It all starts with knowing what the buyer truly values. Spend time understanding their challenges, hopes and limits. Some people care most about cost, while others focus on quality, delivery times, or future results. Once you find their main priorities, shape your offer to show how your solution meets those needs. For example, if saving money is vital to them, talk about how your product lowers total costs and boosts efficiency.

- **Communicate Value Clearly**

A strong offer is not just about numbers on a page. It is about showing how those numbers will help the buyer. Use real data, examples, or stories to prove the impact of your solution. For instance, explain how your product can save time, boost revenue, or reduce downtime. When buyers see the real benefits, they have fewer doubts.

- **Incorporate Flexibility**

Flexible offers often succeed where rigid ones fail. Consider tiered pricing or phased rollouts so the buyer feels they have options. However, plan these choices carefully. You want to guide buyers towards your ideal outcome without losing track of your main objectives.

- **Anchor with Urgency**

People often delay decisions. Adding a sense of urgency can help. This could mean setting a clear deadline or offering a limited-time deal. Be sure this urgency fits the buyer's goals. For example, you might say, "We can offer an extra service if you decide by Friday." Make sure you do not push too hard, or the buyer might walk away.

- **Align Internal Objectives**

Do not forget your own sales targets. Your offer should help increase revenue and build long-term relationships. Think about ways to add value, like cross-sells or upsells, but keep them relevant. By meeting the buyer's needs and your own, you can foster trust and close more deals.

The Art of Timing in Sales

They say timing is everything and in sales, this could not be more true. One well-timed closing move can turn a cautious buyer into a loyal customer. However, choose the wrong moment and you might lose the deal altogether.

Learning when to act starts with spotting signals. Listen for phrases like, "This is exactly what we need," or "Can we begin next week?" These remarks usually mean the buyer is ready. Good timing also depends on solid preparation. If you have done proper research and answered all objections, you will feel more confident about moving forward at the right moment.

But act too soon and the buyer might feel rushed. Wait too long and someone else might step in. The best time to close is when the buyer clearly understands your solution and any worries have been addressed. At that stage, they feel both comfortable and certain.

Confidence also matters. Once you sense it is time, act without hesitation. Use clear language, such as, "Based on everything we have covered, I believe we are ready to move forward. Shall we proceed?" Any sign of doubt on your part might invite the buyer to stall.

Remember, mastering timing is a skill that grows with practice. Study your buyers, prepare thoroughly and speak up at the right moment. This is how you turn fleeting chances into lasting successes.

Overcoming Last-Minute Hesitation

Have you ever watched a deal fall apart at the last moment? It happens when the buyer suddenly has doubts just before signing. Many salespeople dread this, yet there are ways to handle these final uncertainties.

- **Revisit Their Motivations**

Buyers often hesitate because they fear making the wrong choice. Remind them of their main reasons for being interested in the first place. For instance, you might say, "Earlier, you mentioned saving time was your biggest goal. This solution cuts your processing time by 30%, so your team can focus on growth." Bringing them back to their core problem can restore their confidence.

- **Create a Sense of Urgency**

Sometimes, a little nudge is all they need. You could offer a small bonus if they decide soon, like an extra month of support. But do not apply too much pressure. Nobody wants to feel forced.

- **Address Objections Directly**

Ask open-ended questions, such as, "What is making you hesitate?" When they answer, you will know what is holding them back. Offer extra information, case studies, or a customer reference if needed.

- **Reframe the Investment**

The buyer might feel anxious about risk. Show them how your solution is a wise investment. If you can share real numbers about how it saves money or time, do so. You could also offer a trial period or a clear guarantee.

- **Stay Personable, Not Pushy**

No one likes a hard sell at the last minute. Keep the focus on working together to find the right solution. Your goal is to build a long-term relationship, not just close one deal.

Finalising Terms and Securing Commitments

Once you have agreed on terms, it is time to make it official. This step is important because it cements the deal you have worked so hard to build. Why risk misunderstandings or delays at this final hurdle?

Begin by reviewing the key points together—price, timeline and responsibilities. This ensures everyone is on the same page and prevents last-minute surprises. Invite the buyer to share any remaining concerns. If something is unclear, ask for confirmation. You might say, "Just to confirm, we are both clear on the delivery schedule?"

Next, put everything in writing. This is non-negotiable. A written document protects both parties and shows your professionalism. Use clear language that reflects what you discussed. Avoid confusing terms or legal jargon that might cause doubt.

Once the paperwork is ready, take the time to highlight the most important sections. Show the buyer you have kept your word on major points. If the contract is long, offer a brief summary to save time and ensure clarity.

Finally, remember that securing a signature is just the start of a partnership. Give the buyer a clear timeline for what happens next. If installation begins next week, let them know who will be in touch and what they need to prepare. This keeps the momentum going and sets the stage for a positive working relationship.

By focusing on clear communication and careful review, you will build trust and create a strong foundation for future success. Good luck and may your sales journey be both rewarding and profitable!

16. When to Walk Away: Knowing Your Limits

Many salespeople make the mistake of chasing deals that seem valuable at first but do not lead to worthwhile profit. Recognising these weak deals early helps you focus on opportunities that truly benefit your company. But how do you decide if a deal is worth your time and resources?

Start with a profit margin check. Work out the gross profit margin by taking the cost of goods or services away from the revenue, then dividing by the revenue. For instance, if a deal brings in £10,000 but costs £8,000, the margin is 20%. Ask yourself if this meets your organisation's minimum margin. In some fields with tight margins, even a small drop can eat into your earnings.

Next, consider resource demands. This goes beyond money and includes time, staff effort and any missed chances to go after better deals. A deal that needs constant updates or special support can drain your team. Think about a deal that needs loads of extra work from an expert, like a senior developer. It may bring in money, yet if that developer is busy for weeks, you might lose out on bigger projects.

Also look at long-term value. Sometimes, a deal that seems less profitable could provide other benefits, such as a chance to enter a new market or win a well-known client who can give you a reference. Think about whether these gains are worth taking a smaller profit for a while.

To help with these assessments, use tools like deal profitability calculators or CRM systems with forecasting features. By comparing profit margins with resource needs, you can steer clear of deals that cost more than they bring in. In a very competitive sales setting, focusing on profitable deals that fit your aims is a great path to succeed.

Saying "no" can feel odd for anyone in sales. After all, many of us learn to chase every lead and make the most out of each possibility. Yet, looking after your reputation often means knowing when a deal is not a good match and politely turning it down. A sincere refusal can show you are honest, which builds trust and keeps the door open for future contact.

When you must refuse a deal, explain your reasoning in a fair and kind manner. You could say, "I appreciate the time we spent looking at your needs. Right now, I feel our solution may not meet your requirements and I do not want to overpromise." This shows you care about the client's best interests instead of only your own.

It often helps to suggest another way forward. You might recommend a different service or leave room to talk again if their needs change: "While we might not suit your needs now, I would be glad to speak again when our services match what you are looking for." Being helpful, even when refusing, can leave a lasting, positive effect.

Keep your tone polite and friendly. You never want your "no" to seem cold or dismissive. Aim to show you want the best outcome for the other person. In the end, saying "no" is not a defeat—it is a plan that saves your resources and preserves trust. People will remember your honesty and may return when the time is right.

Confidence in sales is not just about introducing products or sealing deals. It is also about knowing when to walk away. This may sound unusual in a high-pressure job, but it can be good for your credibility and mental health.

Walking away shows you respect yourself and your work. Some believe every deal must be closed. But chasing deals that do not make money or feel toxic can waste time and lower how others see your expertise. When you decide to leave a deal that clashes with your aims or values, you show that your work is valuable. This boosts your reputation, since you appear more selective and truthful, not desperate.

On a personal level, walking away can protect you from stress. Sales can be tough and full of risks. Not every deal is worth the hassle. Accepting that you should pick your battles helps you stay calm and see that success comes from quality rather than quantity. This view strengthens your confidence, letting you focus on deals that suit your strengths.

It can also help during negotiations. If the other side realises you are ready to leave, they may see you as a helpful expert, not a pushy seller. This sometimes makes them rethink their offers and possibly make better proposals. Oddly enough, being willing to step away may lead them to move closer.

Walking away is not about being arrogant. Instead, it is about keeping control over your decisions and priorities. It lets you protect your mind and grow your reputation in a positive way, which is vital in sales.

In sales, not every lead will become a deal and not every business relationship will continue. But how you end these connections can shape your future. Knowing how to finish on good terms is an important skill.

Show politeness, say thank you and keep things mutual. Always show you understand the other party's views, even if the deal ends. Try to leave them feeling heard. Clear and honest communication is key. You might say, "I understand your concerns and hope we can still work together later."

Gratitude goes a long way. A simple thank you for their effort can help you both part on a better note. You might also remain a resource by sharing ideas or offers even after the deal ends. This way, you stay in their good books.

Finally, record the details in a proper way. Send a follow-up message to confirm what was discussed, show your thanks and mention that you are open to contact in the future. This shows you care about the relationship and value their time.

In sales, relationships matter. How you end a chapter often decides whether it can open again later. By closing deals politely and looking ahead, you might turn a dead end into a chance for success in the future.

Losing a deal can feel like a big let-down. However, missed deals can teach you valuable lessons. Every deal that falls apart can reveal what went wrong and how to improve. A detailed look at your mistakes is a must for growth.

Start by being totally honest. Do not blame high prices or stiff competition alone. Ask: Did I really understand the buyer's concerns? Did I prove my service's value well? Was my pitch at the right time? By asking these questions, you find where you can do better.

Working with others can help. Get input from teammates who may notice things you missed. Sometimes you are too close to the deal to see errors. Also, consider asking the client for feedback, as it might show you how your rivals outperformed you or where you fell short.

Use what you learn to tweak your next approach. You might change your presentation, listen more closely, or react quicker to market changes. Every loss can make you stronger if you use it to adjust your strategies.

Remember, you do not have to close every deal to be a true sales expert. The real goal is to learn from the losses and refine your skills for the future.

17. Maintaining Long-Term Relationships: Winning Beyond the Sale

Many focus all their energy on winning new clients. But is that always the best strategy? Building strong relationships with current customers often brings even greater rewards.

Securing new customers can be expensive. Studies show it costs much more to gain a new client than to keep an existing one. Meanwhile, a satisfied customer usually returns for additional purchases. They may spend more and show less resistance when you offer new services or products.

Moreover, happy clients become your greatest supporters. Their loyalty can lead to referrals and testimonials that attract new prospects. A positive recommendation from someone who trusts your business is far more powerful than any advertisement.

Continuing to serve existing clients also gives you a competitive edge. As they get to know you and your solutions, they grow more comfortable sharing their changing needs. When you can offer tailored answers, you become hard to replace. Over time, this makes it difficult for competitors to lure them away.

In a world that favours quick wins, it can be tempting to chase new deals. Yet real success comes from playing the long game. Repeat business turns simple transactions into partnerships and your clients into allies. This sets the stage for steady growth, even in the toughest markets.

Mastering the Follow-Up
Consistent follow-up is vital in sales, but it must strike a balance. Nobody likes feeling hounded. Buyers today receive countless emails, calls and messages. How can your follow-up stand out?

- **Adopt a Buyer-Centric Mindset**

Always ask yourself: "What's in it for them?" A buyer wants a solution to their problem, not just another sales pitch. Use your follow-ups to show how your product or service meets their unique needs. Share helpful tips, success stories, or market insights that speak to their goals.

- **Use Different Channels**

Don't rely on only one form of communication. Combine emails, phone calls, social media messages and handwritten notes. Mixing it up prevents your contacts from feeling overwhelmed and keeps your outreach fresh.

- **Respect Their Timeline**

Following up too often can show impatience. Ask early on when they plan to make a decision and honour that timeframe. This approach reduces the risk of bombarding them before they are ready.

- **Be Helpful, Not Pushy**

Instead of asking, "Have you decided yet?" offer something valuable. Perhaps send a case study or a brief article that could guide them. This keeps the focus on their needs and positions you as an advisor.

- **Set Clear Expectations**

End each contact with a next step. For example, "I'll call you next Friday—is that convenient?" This prevents confusion and ensures both sides know what to expect.

Staying in touch is not just about closing a sale; it's about earning trust. By providing real value and respecting boundaries, you become a helpful partner rather than a persistent seller.

Gaining Value from Feedback

In sales, feedback is often overlooked. Yet insights from customers can refine your approach and improve future results. Whether you close a sale or lose it, learning from each experience is priceless.

Begin by asking the right questions. After a deal, schedule a feedback session. Keep the tone friendly and curious. Ask questions like, "What made you choose us?" or "Did anything nearly stop you from buying?" If you lost the deal, you might ask, "What could we have done differently?"

Listen carefully and record what you learn. You may start to see patterns. For instance, if many people mention unclear pricing, you know this is an area to fix. If competitors seem more appealing, figure out why and adjust your pitch to stand out.

Acting on feedback is just as important as collecting it. If customers are confused about product features, create clearer sales materials or give a sharper presentation. Share these findings with your team so everyone can improve.

Feedback also confirms what you're doing right. If buyers praise a certain approach, emphasise it in your next meetings. Finally, thank your customers for their honesty. Showing gratitude strengthens your relationship and makes them more likely to help you in the future.

Remember, sales success can vanish if you become complacent. Treat every bit of feedback as a chance to get better. This mindset keeps you moving forward, even in the most demanding sales environments.

Building Trust Through Consistency

Consistency is the backbone of trust. Buyers have many choices, so why should they pick you? One reason is your reliability. If you promise to send a quote by Friday, make sure it arrives no later than Thursday. Doing what you say you will do proves you are dependable.

Trust builds slowly. Small actions, repeated over time, show that you deliver on your promises. This leads to loyalty, which is a powerful advantage in crowded markets. When clients know they can count on you, they return—not just because of your product, but because of your proven track record.

Consistency also benefits your team. Managers, colleagues and partners will notice you always follow through. This reputation often leads to more opportunities and support.

In the end, keeping your word is not just a professional duty—it's a wise strategy. When people trust you, they choose to stay with you. Trust is hard to earn but very easy to lose. Make reliability your competitive edge by fulfilling every commitment, big or small.

Turning Buyers into Advocates

Satisfied buyers are a huge asset in sales. They can move beyond being regular customers and become enthusiastic supporters of your brand. But how can you turn buyers into true advocates?

Start by exceeding their expectations. Anyone can promise quick delivery, but can you add extra value? When customers feel understood and respected, they become loyal. This loyalty often inspires them to spread the word about your business.

Keep the relationship going after the sale. Regular check-ins and exclusive updates show you still care. Stay genuine and offer information they can use in everyday life. For example, if they bought a cybersecurity service, share industry tips or a short guide on new data protection rules.

Empower them to share their experiences. Tools like referral programmes or ready-made social media posts can help. Remember, however, that advocacy should feel natural, not forced. Authentic reviews and testimonials are far more convincing than scripted quotes.

Never forget to say thank you. Recognise or reward your advocates for their support. A small gesture of gratitude can go a long way in keeping the relationship positive.

In tough sales environments, word-of-mouth is gold. A referral from a trusted friend often carries more weight than any sales pitch. When your customers become your advocates, they help your business grow faster and stronger. They become part of your success story and that's something no competitor can match.

18. Remote Negotiations: Techniques for the Virtual World

Remote negotiations are now a major part of modern sales, especially as more people rely on virtual communication. But how can you build trust and close deals from behind a screen?

One major challenge in remote negotiations is the lack of personal connection. Meeting face-to-face gives you chances to build rapport through small talk and body language. Online, these moments are often shorter or feel less natural. Without trust, negotiations can stall and misunderstandings might happen more often.

Technical issues also make things difficult. Weak internet connections, glitches in audio, or problems with software can interrupt conversations and cause frustration. Even one small error can break the flow and lower the sense of professionalism. It can be hard to get back on track once your focus is lost.

Another problem is the limited ability to read non-verbal cues. On video calls, it is harder to notice the small changes in someone's facial expressions or posture. These clues help you sense how the other person feels. Missing them can lead to confusion or missed chances to adapt your approach.

Time zone differences add yet another hurdle. In global sales, finding a meeting time that works for everyone can slow down the process and extend the negotiation cycle. This delay may put you at a disadvantage if your competitors act faster.

To overcome these obstacles, you must use strong communication skills and prepare well. Practise using virtual tools until you know them by heart. The more comfortable you feel, the better you can guide negotiations and see positive results.

Have you ever struggled to connect with someone over a video call? In the fast-paced world of sales, finding ways to build rapport online is crucial. When meeting in person, a welcoming handshake or a friendly smile helps you bond right away. But in a virtual setting, you need a more focused approach.

First, pay attention to your surroundings. A neat, uncluttered background shows that you take the meeting seriously. Good lighting and a decent camera make it easier for others to see your expressions. Eye contact is still important online, so try to look directly into the camera when you speak. This helps the other person feel like you are looking at them.

Non-verbal cues also matter. A warm smile sets a positive tone. Hand gestures can highlight key ideas and make you seem more energetic. Nodding along when someone else is talking shows respect and interest, which encourages them to keep talking.

Preparation is another key step. Before the call, learn about the person or company you are meeting. Finding a shared interest or mentioning something positive about their work can start the conversation on a friendly note.

Next, remember to keep your energy levels high. Speak with enthusiasm and vary your tone of voice. This holds the other person's attention and helps them feel motivated. End your call with a warm thank-you for their time, leaving them with a sense of value and respect.

When video calls are done right, they can feel just as strong as in-person meetings. By focusing on visuals, preparation and engagement, you can build trust and succeed in any online setting.

In today's competitive sales world, the right technology makes a big difference. The best tools support smooth communication, teamwork and data-sharing. Video conferencing platforms like Zoom, Microsoft Teams, or Google Meet allow you to share screens and watch body language in real time. Adding virtual whiteboards like Miro or MURAL can help teams solve problems together more easily.

Document-sharing tools such as DocuSign or PandaDoc are also useful. They let both sides sign contracts right away, which speeds up the negotiation process. Meanwhile, Customer Relationship Management (CRM) systems like Salesforce or HubSpot store all your data and past conversations in one place. This helps you enter meetings well-prepared.

Yet even the best tools cannot fix every issue. Technical problems remain a risk, so test your setup beforehand. It is wise to have a backup plan ready, like a second meeting link or a phone conference line. You do not want to lose momentum if your main tool fails.

Another concern is the loss of human connection. Virtual calls can feel cold, so try to warm them up by starting with a bit of friendly chatter. Keep your tone open and make eye contact with the camera. Small efforts like these remind the other person that you value their time.

Miscommunication is also common. Typing short messages or sending emails can lead to errors, so summarise the main points at the end of each call. This helps ensure that everyone understands the agreement and is ready for the next step.

Finally, remove distractions. Close unnecessary web pages, silence notifications and ask all participants to focus. Virtual negotiations require clear thinking and good preparation. Mastering these tools and habits helps you compete in sales and offer value to your customers.

In the busy world of sales, non-verbal communication still plays a crucial role, even when you cannot meet in person. Simple signals like a welcoming smile or a calm voice can build trust and reveal unspoken thoughts.

In video meetings, your appearance and background make the first impression. A clean, bright space shows professionalism, while wearing the right clothes sets the tone for the conversation. On camera, facial expressions matter more than ever. Try to stay relaxed and smile often. Aim to look into the camera so the other person feels seen.

Listening carefully is also important. Nodding, tilting forward and saying short phrases like "Yes" or "I see" show you are paying attention. Notice any changes in the other person's voice or expression. A quick frown or a sudden silence could mean worry or doubt.

On phone calls, you cannot rely on visuals. In that case, your voice becomes the main way to express feeling. Speak clearly and with a steady pace and remember to smile as you talk. Even over the phone, a simple smile affects how your voice sounds. Pay attention to quiet pauses or sudden changes in tone—these may indicate questions or hesitations.

The secret to using non-verbal techniques in virtual negotiations is to be purposeful. When you are not in the same room, every small detail can matter. By focusing on how you present yourself and how you read others, you can build trust, sense the mood of the conversation and guide remote negotiations to successful outcomes.

19. Negotiating as a Team: Leveraging Collective Strengths

In the fast-paced world of sales, negotiation often feels like a battle between two people. Yet, there are times when bringing a team to the table can have clear advantages. A strong team can combine different types of expertise, make better decisions and show buyers a sense of unity and skill. Knowing when to negotiate as a team and how to organise the right structure is vital for lasting success.

Team negotiation is especially useful in complex, high-stakes deals. When several parties are involved—such as in large government contracts or major corporate agreements—a group approach can handle different parts of the negotiation at once. Imagine one person focusing on price, another tackling technical issues and a third dealing with legal details. By dividing the work, nobody is overloaded and every part of the deal gets proper attention.

Negotiating as a team also helps when dealing with cultural or hierarchical differences. In many industries and cultures, having a senior leader in the room shows dedication and seriousness. Including experts or decision-makers can reassure your buyer that you have the knowledge and authority to finalise the deal.

However, simply gathering a team is not enough. You must define clear roles. First, decide who will lead the negotiation. This lead negotiator guides the conversation, keeps the discussion on track and listens carefully to the client's needs. Other team members should cover specific areas, such as technical insights or taking notes. You may even have a silent observer who studies the room and shares feedback during breaks.

Preparation is the key to success. Meet beforehand to agree on shared goals, talking points and possible back-up plans if the negotiation takes an unexpected turn. By rehearsing scenarios, your team can reduce confusion and stay confident once you face the buyer.

When done well, team negotiation gives you a stronger hand to play and helps you stand out from your competitors. It can make difficult deals easier to close and help your organisation gain a better reputation in the market.

Defining Clear Roles for Team Negotiations

In a high-pressure sales meeting, it is important that your team works like a well-tuned machine. Everyone should know their part and stick to it. Clear roles remove overlap, boost performance and give your team the confidence to handle any question that comes up.

- **The Lead Negotiator**

The lead negotiator is the centre of any team negotiation. This person takes charge of the conversation, keeps the dialogue flowing and focuses on the client's main goals. They must stay calm under stress and have a firm grasp on all parts of the deal. This includes pricing, timelines and any give-and-take arrangements.

Good people skills are also critical for this role. The lead negotiator should quickly read the room, build rapport and adjust strategies when needed.

- **The Subject Expert**

A subject expert helps the lead negotiator by offering deep knowledge of the product, service, or solution at hand. Their job is to clarify technical details, manage objections and highlight your value. This expert must be careful not to use too much detail, which can confuse the buyer and slow down the negotiation.

- **The Observer**

Often overlooked, the observer's role is to watch everything that happens. They quietly study what the buyer says and does, noting body language and shifts in tone. After the meeting, they share insights on what worked well and what needs improving. The observer stays silent during talks unless asked for input, so they do not break the flow of conversation.

- **The Framework in Action**

Before any negotiation, plan a briefing to decide who will fill each role and set out what is expected. Make sure you match people's strengths with the job they do best. It can also help to rotate roles from time to time, so team members learn new skills and become more flexible. In sales, careful planning and proper role assignment can be the secret to winning more deals.

Achieving Internal Alignment

Before you step into a sales negotiation, your team must be in sync. If you show up unprepared or with mixed messages, you risk damaging trust and losing control of the conversation. This is why proper internal alignment—where your team agrees on strategy, goals and boundaries—is so important.

Start by gathering everyone involved in the deal: sales, marketing, finance, operations and leadership. Go over the buyer's requirements, your top value points and any possible sticking points. These might include price limits or product limits. Make sure everyone knows their role and understands the plan.

Next, define your walk-away points. It is common for people on the same team to have different views on how far to bend, especially on price. By agreeing on clear boundaries, you allow the negotiation lead to act with confidence.

Also, think about any likely buyer objections. Maybe they worry about long delivery times or strict contract rules. Prepare a single, united response to these questions, so your team will all say the same thing. Different answers from different people can harm your credibility.

Encourage open, honest discussion before the negotiation. It is better to argue things out behind closed doors than to clash in front of the buyer. Once you have a shared plan, present a united front. This will show the buyer that your organisation is professional, trustworthy and ready to deliver what is promised.

Presenting a Unified Front

In a high-stakes deal, buyers can sense if your team is not on the same page. Mixed messages or contradictory statements can quickly break trust and hurt your position. If you want to close the deal, it is vital to show a unified front.

Start by setting up a strategy meeting with everyone on your side. Agree on the key issues, your overall goals and how you will handle possible questions or objections. Sort out who will lead the talk, who will answer technical queries and who will negotiate prices or terms. When everyone knows their role, you reduce the chance of confusion later.

Then, align on your main messages. You can use a simple script or a set of talking points that address the buyer's challenges and how your solution helps them. Keep your language clear and do not overwhelm the buyer with too much information.

During the negotiation, stay in touch with your teammates. Some teams use digital messaging tools or take short pauses to reconnect. This is a good way to handle new, unexpected questions without stepping on each other's toes. If you do not have a ready answer, it is better to take a moment to confirm than to share inconsistent details.

Lastly, hold a short debrief after each negotiation session. Review what was said, check that everyone is still in agreement and decide on any new tactics for the next round. This will keep your team strong and prevent mistakes from repeating.

A well-coordinated team builds confidence in the buyer's mind. Buyers are more likely to trust a group that speaks with one voice and looks prepared. By showing unity, you improve your odds of making the sale and creating a lasting impression.

Learning Through Post-Negotiation Reviews

Negotiation is not over once the deal is won or lost. In the world of sales, teams grow stronger by looking back and analysing what went right and what could be done better. Post-negotiation reviews are a powerful tool for learning and improving.

These reviews should feel safe and open. They are not about blaming someone for a mistake. Instead, they help you spot how to be more effective next time. For example, did the team fully understand the client's needs? Did anyone miss a chance to highlight key data? How could communication be improved?

Feedback is vital. Encourage everyone to share their views honestly. Talk about what worked well, but also focus on what needs polishing. Perhaps there was a point where the team lost focus, or a buyer question was not answered correctly. By facing these issues and learning from them, you make sure the same problems do not happen again.

It also helps to keep written records. Make short summaries after each negotiation and store them in a shared place. New team members can learn from these notes and experienced members can revisit them for ideas. Over time, your organisation will build a powerful library of best practices.

When you follow these steps, your team develops a mindset of growth and flexibility. In the challenging world of sales, this is crucial for standing out. A team that is always improving will be ready for anything the buyer might throw at them. Keep reflecting, keep learning and keep winning.

20. Dealing with Difficult Personalities: Handling the Toughest Buyers

Have you ever dealt with buyers who are so challenging that you feel stuck? In sales, understanding different types of difficult buyers is vital. By adjusting your approach, you can turn tough interactions into productive conversations.

- **The Aggressive Buyer**

Aggressive buyers may dominate discussions, question your expertise, or demand unrealistic terms. They often create a tense atmosphere that makes it hard to build a relationship.

To manage this, stay calm and collected. Focus on facts and value and avoid getting drawn into arguments. Listen carefully to their points, then guide the conversation towards teamwork. You could say, "I understand your main concerns. Let's see how we can solve them together." This phrase shows respect while lowering their guard.

- **The Indecisive Buyer**

Do you know someone who always hesitates before making a decision? Indecisive buyers often worry about choosing the wrong product or service. This can slow down the sales process.

To help them move forward, simplify their options. Offer only a few clear choices and back them up with data or success stories. You might ask, "What is your top priority right now?" This question helps you understand their needs so you can focus on the solution that suits them best.

- **The Dismissive Buyer**

Some buyers show little interest or act as though your input is not valuable. This can make you feel overlooked, but patience is key.

Build credibility by sharing relevant success stories or industry examples. Ask open-ended questions to spark a real discussion, such as, "What is your biggest challenge in this area?" If they respond, you have a chance to show you care and have useful insights.

When you recognise these difficult behaviours and respond with empathy, you can turn challenging moments into opportunities. Staying flexible and understanding can help you close more deals and earn the buyer's trust.

Aggression in High-Pressure Environments

Sales can be stressful and aggression often appears when people feel frustrated or misunderstood. Knowing how to calm aggressive behaviour is crucial if you want to keep things professional and productive.

Calming Techniques

- **Stay Composed:**

Keep a steady tone of voice and avoid using defensive gestures. Calm breathing signals that you are in control.

- **Empathy and Active Listening:**

Show that you understand their feelings. Saying, "I can see how this might be frustrating," can ease the tension.

- **Pause and Reflect:**

If aggression flares up, take a moment of silence before you answer. This helps you respond more thoughtfully.

Strategies to Redirect Aggressive Behaviours

- **Focus on Solutions:**

Encourage the other person to discuss possible fixes by asking, "What outcome would work best for you?" This switches the tone from confrontation to cooperation.

- **Use Positive Reinforcement:**

Thank them for pointing out problems or concerns. You could say, "I appreciate you highlighting that. Let's find a way to address it."

- **Set Boundaries Respectfully:**

Remain polite when establishing limits. For instance, "I'd like to keep this respectful so we can reach a good outcome," can calm heated exchanges.

By using these techniques, you can steer negative energy towards understanding and problem-solving.

Identifying and Countering Manipulation

High-pressure sales environments often involve subtle manipulation. Have you ever noticed someone using guilt or fear to push you into a quick decision?

Stay alert to phrases that rush or shame you into agreement. A client might say, "Your competitor is cheaper," to make you offer discounts you cannot afford. When you sense manipulation, remain calm. Avoid reacting emotionally and instead ask clarifying questions like, "Why is this timeline so urgent?" This shifts the focus to facts, not feelings.

Set firm boundaries by politely stating what you can and cannot do. If a client insists on an immediate discount, respond with, "I understand your concern, but I need to confirm costs before I can commit." Confidence in your expertise is your best defence. Manipulators often target self-doubt, so remind yourself of your skills and knowledge.

Working with Reluctant or Skeptical Buyers

It can be daunting to face buyers who are distrustful or cautious. Yet, if you handle them well, they might become your greatest supporters.

- **Understand Their Perspective**
Ask simple, open-ended questions like, "What worries you about this choice?" This helps you uncover hidden fears or past experiences that shaped their hesitation.

- **Build Credibility**
Prove that you and your product are reliable by sharing stories of real success. Provide data or testimonials from clients with similar needs. When you back your claims with facts, buyers feel safer.

- **Empathise Rather Than Persuade**

Show that you truly hear their concerns. A phrase like, "I see why you might feel unsure," can make them feel respected. This reduces defences and opens the door to better dialogue.

- **Offer Low-Risk Options**

Some buyers need extra assurance. Suggest a pilot programme, free trial, or smaller contract first. If it works out, they can then commit to a larger deal.

- **Adapt Your Pace**

Not every buyer wants to move quickly. Let them have the time and details they need. Stay patient and avoid any pressure tactics that might scare them away.

When you show genuine care and deliver real results, sceptical buyers start seeing you as a partner, not just a salesperson.

Turning Difficult Buyers into Loyal Partners

Some buyers might seem overly critical or even hostile at first. However, they often have deep concerns or past disappointments. By addressing these worries with empathy and honesty, you can build strong partnerships.

- **Discover the Root Cause**

Why are they so sceptical or aggressive? Listen closely to uncover their unmet expectations or bad experiences. This shows you respect their feelings and might reveal what they truly want.

- **Be Transparent and Consistent**

Difficult buyers often test you. If you promise to do something, follow through. Be proactive in your communication. Even small actions, done well, create the trust they crave.

- **Stay Flexible**

A rigid approach can make tough buyers shut down. Adjust your product or service to fit their goals. When they see you are open to their ideas, they are more likely to cooperate.

- **Maintain Your Resolve**

It is not easy to win over a tough buyer. Yet, these challenging situations often lead to the strongest relationships. Once they trust you, they may become your most loyal customers.

When a difficult buyer transforms into a loyal partner, the benefits go far beyond a single deal. They may return for more business, recommend you to others and share valuable feedback. Each time you handle a challenging situation, you improve your skills and deepen your relationships. After all, every tough buyer is an opportunity for growth and success.

21. Case Studies: Real-World Negotiation Success Stories

High-pressure sales often involve intense negotiations that can make or break a deal. Each negotiation holds unique challenges, but there are common strategies that help achieve success. Below are some examples that show how different scenarios demand composure and creativity.

Negotiating Public Sector Frameworks

Securing a public sector framework agreement with the Royal Armouries was a high-stakes project. It not only provided immediate revenue but also opened doors to other organisations needing long-term IT solutions. The main challenge was the need to follow strict public sector rules while giving the client tailored services.

To solve this, the team used clear and constant communication. They made sure every step followed the law but still offered flexibility. In the end, they locked in a legally compliant agreement that guaranteed recurring business for several years.

Technology Procurement with Tight Deadlines

A global retailer needed a multi-site telephony solution in just three months. This tight schedule put everyone under pressure. The critical negotiation focused on getting first access to hardware from a technology vendor.

By highlighting a strong partnership and sharing accurate forecasts, the team convinced the vendor that both sides stood to gain. This sped up the procurement process, met the retailer's deadline and strengthened trust between the two companies.

Crisis Negotiation: Service Recovery After a Security Breach

When a cybersecurity breach shook an enterprise client, they needed urgent upgrades to their systems. Negotiations covered the pricing of fast deployment for CloudStrike's threat detection tools. The client faced budget worries but needed top-notch protection.

A tiered pricing approach eased some of the cost pressure. Extended service contracts also spread out expenses. As a result, the client regained security and confidence in a cost-effective way.

Large-Scale Training Programme Delivery

Peloton required a global training programme across three continents. Different markets had varying needs, which made alignment tough. The team used cultural awareness and flexible planning. They adapted each agreement to local preferences while sticking to overall goals.

The outcome was a successful training launch, with excellent engagement scores in every region.

Shared Strategies in High-Stakes Negotiations

Across these stories, a few strategies rise to the top:

- **Empathy and Active Listening**
Truly hearing people's concerns can lead to surprising solutions.

- **Data-Driven Approaches**
Backing ideas with facts builds trust and reduces doubt.

- **Proactive Problem-Solving**
Addressing concerns before they arise shows true expertise.

By combining these strategies, sales professionals can navigate even the toughest deals. Each step in a deal—such as balancing client needs, handling legal requirements and juggling market pressures—should fit together like a puzzle. Over time, three lessons stand out: adaptability, patience and strategic thinking.

Adaptability: The Art of Pivoting

High-stakes negotiations can change at any moment. Clients might shift their focus or competitors may jump in with a new offer. How do you stay prepared? Adaptability.

I once worked with a public sector client whose budget changed mid-negotiation. Rather than give up, I quickly adjusted our proposal and switched to a phased plan. This helped us meet their needs without breaking their new budget. Adaptability is not a weakness; it shows strength and reliability.

Patience: The Quiet Power

Complex deals usually take time. Patience is vital, especially when you must satisfy legal teams and multiple stakeholders. Moving too fast can cause mistakes or push clients to feel uneasy.

In one framework agreement, I spent months fine-tuning contract terms with the client's legal team. The end result was a win-win deal that set us up for long-term success. Patience helps you see the big picture and allows trust to grow naturally.

Strategic Thinking: The Master Plan

Every major deal demands a plan. You need to map out key decision-makers, guess potential objections and study the competition. A strong strategy looks beyond a single win to the wider benefits for everyone involved.

When working with education customers, I often show how our solutions serve both short-term needs and long-term goals. This approach proves I understand their world and helps me earn their trust.

High-pressure sales can feel like a battlefield. Adaptability, patience and strategic thinking become your armour. Use these tools and you can succeed even when the odds seem stacked against you.

Handling Price Objections: Showcasing Value

Overcoming price objections is a critical skill in sales. An IT salesperson once sold premium cybersecurity software to mid-sized firms. The software cost more than its rivals and prospects often pushed back on price.

One prospect, a financial services firm, worried they could get "similar results" with a cheaper product. Instead of pushing back right away, the salesperson listened closely. They learned that the true worry was meeting new regulations and staying safe from data breaches.

To reframe the conversation, the salesperson explained the software's powerful threat detection tools. They showed how a 40% drop in breach risk could safeguard reputations and how automated compliance features saved IT teams about 10 hours per week. A story about another client who avoided a costly breach sealed the deal. Finally, a short pilot gave the prospect low-risk proof of the software's benefits. Within three months, the client saw real returns and became a loyal partner.

This example shows that overcoming price barriers is not about lowering the cost. Instead, it is about proving the product's worth.

Winning Over a Difficult Buyer

Turning a sceptical buyer into a loyal customer can be one of the most rewarding experiences in sales. A few years ago, I encountered a buyer who had been let down by a previous vendor. They didn't trust salespeople and refused to talk at length.

I responded with empathy. I listened carefully to their struggles and did not argue. This small act built trust. I followed up with helpful resources, including a case study that matched their situation. Over time, the buyer saw I understood their problems and wasn't just chasing a commission.

A breakthrough happened when I proposed a phased trial to reduce their risk. I also connected them with a current client who shared a positive, honest review. The buyer saw we cared about their success and agreed to test our product. Within six months, they expanded their order and became an enthusiastic advocate for our company.

This story proves that stubborn buyers can transform into allies when you show patience and genuine concern for their needs.

Navigating Multi-Stakeholder Deals

Selling to large organisations often involves many stakeholders. Each group may have different goals, which can feel like herding cats. In one case, whilst working as a BDM I pitched a cybersecurity solution to a big university. The IT team wanted strong endpoint protection, the finance team worried about cost, the legal team needed GDPR compliance and the academic leaders wanted easy access for students and staff.

I made a point of meeting with each group separately to understand their needs. For the IT department, stressing the solution's ability to grow over time. For finance, I provided a cost-benefit analysis. For legal, I arranged an external compliance audit. For academic leaders, I suggested a pilot phase to test real-world impact.

I then held a workshop for all stakeholders. I showed how each group's concerns were handled. By focusing on common goals, such as protecting the university's reputation and avoiding disruptions for staff and students, everyone agreed on a three-year contract. The outcome was improved security, strong compliance and user-friendly operations.

What can we learn here? Large deals require patience, empathy and a knack for creating unity. When you address each group's priorities and remind them of their shared interests, success becomes much more likely.

Negotiations in sales can be challenging, but they are also full of possibilities. With empathy, data-driven insights and open communication, you can solve problems and build lasting partnerships. Keep these lessons in mind and you will soon handle even the most complex deals with confidence.

22. Common Pitfalls to Avoid: Lessons from Experience

Over-promising and under-delivering can be one of the most harmful traps in sales and negotiation. Have you ever felt pressured to promise more than you can actually provide? In the moment, it might feel tempting to say "yes" to everything just to close a deal. However, this short-term victory often creates long-term problems when you cannot meet the expectations you set.

When promises are broken, trust begins to slip away. This trust is the foundation of every successful business relationship. The disappointment felt by clients or partners can quickly spread, especially within close-knit industries. Before you know it, one broken promise could affect not just your current deal but also your future opportunities.

Another issue caused by over-promising is the strain it places on your own team. Imagine how your colleagues feel when they are asked to do the impossible in a short amount of time. It leads to stress, lower-quality work and frustration. Over time, this can harm your entire organisation's morale.

What is the best way to avoid this mistake? Instead of trying to "win at any cost," focus on honest communication. Be clear about what you can truly achieve with the given resources. If you under-promise and then over-deliver, you will not only fulfil expectations but often surpass them. This approach helps build a reputation for reliability, which is vital for long-term success in sales.

It is also important to remember that true success is not just about winning one deal. Instead, it's about building lasting relationships. By being truthful and meeting your commitments, you earn credibility and loyalty. These qualities lead to repeat business and positive word-of-mouth. In the end, taking the time to manage expectations pays off far more than any quick gain ever could.

Misreading a buyer's top priorities is another risky error many salespeople make. Have you ever assumed that price must be the most important factor, only to discover that the client actually cares more about speed or reliability? It is easy to guess what we think someone wants, but this approach can cause serious problems.

When you assume incorrectly, you create a pitch that might not match your client's real needs. They may feel ignored or misunderstood. This can harm trust and block the path to a successful deal.

It is also a mistake to rely solely on past trends or industry norms. While these can offer some insight, each buyer is unique. A one-size-fits-all approach may leave buyers thinking you do not see their specific challenges.

So, how do you avoid this pitfall? Ask questions, listen closely and then confirm what you have heard. For instance, you might say, "What goal is most important for you right now?" or "Which problems are causing you the most trouble?" Take notes, repeat back key points and check if you understood them correctly. By doing this, you can tailor your offer to match exactly what the buyer values.

When your proposal addresses the buyer's real concerns, you show that you are a true problem-solver. This helps build trust and increases your chances of closing the deal. After all, people want to feel seen and heard. Focusing on their true priorities, rather than your own assumptions, sets you apart in any competitive market.

Another common mistake is putting too much emphasis on price. Of course, cost does matter. But if you talk only about price, you might miss your chance to show the full worth of your product or service.

When everything centres on price, your client may never learn about the features that make your solution special—such as superior technology or outstanding customer support. If price is the only focus, buyers might believe your product is cheap for a reason, or they might not realise the broader advantages you offer.

Focusing too heavily on cost can also turn your service into a commodity. In such a race to the bottom, unique benefits get lost. Margins suffer and your brand's image may slip. Instead, lead with the value your product brings. How does it solve problems? How does it create long-term savings or reduce risks? Answering these questions helps the buyer see why your offering is worth the investment.

Remember, people rarely buy just because the price is right. They want solutions to their problems and partners they can trust. Staying confident in the value you provide is key. When you believe in your solution, others are more likely to believe in it too.

Ignoring non-verbal signals is another costly error. Have you ever been in a meeting where someone's words said "yes," but their body language screamed "no"? Actions often speak louder than words and reading these cues is vital in sales.

For example, when someone crosses their arms or leans away, they might feel uneasy—even if they say they agree. Or if their tone of voice sounds flat, they could be bored or unsure. Paying attention to these details helps you adapt your message and ask clarifying questions.

If you fail to notice non-verbal clues, you may push forward with a pitch that does not resonate. Over time, constantly missing these signals can damage your relationships. People may think you do not care enough to really understand them.

To excel, develop a skill for observing body language, facial expressions and tone. Create a comfortable space where clients feel free to share doubts and concerns. By truly listening and responding to what is left unsaid, you can uncover hidden objections, offer better solutions and strengthen trust. After all, sometimes the most important messages are the ones not spoken out loud.

Finally, rushing the close is a mistake that can ruin even the most promising opportunities. Have you ever felt so eager to finalise a deal that you tried to close too soon? Buyers often sense that hurry and it can make them hesitate or back away.

When you rush, you might ignore or gloss over their concerns. This tells the buyer that their needs may not be your top priority. Pushing too hard can break rapport and make you seem desperate, which damages your credibility.

The best way to find the right moment to close is to pay close attention. Look out for signs that the buyer is ready, such as enthusiastic agreement or specific questions about using your product. If the buyer still seems unsure, address their questions and reassure them. Open-ended questions are very useful here. They help you spot doubts, solve problems and show genuine concern for the client's situation.

Closing at just the right time not only secures the deal but also lays the groundwork for a long-lasting partnership. In a world where trust matters, you want clients to feel good about choosing you. By respecting their journey and earning their confidence, you create satisfied customers who will recommend you to others.

In sales, each of these common errors can weaken your results. Yet with careful attention, empathy and a willingness to learn, you can avoid these pitfalls. Focus on building genuine connections, identifying real needs and highlighting the unique value you offer. Approach every deal with honesty and patience. This way, you create success that lasts for both you and your clients.

23. The Role of Ethics in Negotiation

Have you ever felt pressured to hit a sales target so badly that you considered bending the truth? In the fast-paced world of sales, it can be tempting to cut corners. Yet, holding on to your integrity can set you apart from competitors and keep your reputation strong for years to come.

Why Ethics Matter in Sales

Ethical selling is not just about being nice. It is a smart strategy that builds trust and respect. When customers feel valued and treated fairly, they tend to return. They may even spread the word about your honesty to friends and colleagues. Trust, once earned, acts like a savings account—you make deposits through ethical actions and risk withdrawals with deceit. If you damage that trust, fixing it can be very difficult.

Your reputation is everything in sales. With online reviews and social media, a single bad experience can quickly reach many people. You might win a few short-term deals through dishonesty, but you risk harming your good name. Unethical deals often fall apart, leaving you with angry clients and tarnished relationships.

Common Unethical Behaviours

• **Misrepresentation**
Exaggerating a product's abilities or hiding flaws may lead to quick sales, but it creates unhappy customers and possible legal trouble later.

• **High-Pressure Tactics**
Pushing buyers with scare tactics like "Offer ends today!" may force a sale, but it breeds regret and often causes returns or poor reviews.

• **Overpromising**
Promising impossible results just to close a deal leads to disappointment and erodes your credibility.

• **Concealing Costs**
Leaving out important fees or unfavourable terms can seal a deal, but it destroys trust when buyers realise the true costs.

• **Criticising Colleagues or Competitors**
Speaking badly of others may seem like a way to win, but it usually backfires. It makes you appear unprofessional and untrustworthy.

Avoiding Unethical Practices

• Stay Transparent
Always share accurate information about your product, its cost and any limits. Customers appreciate honesty and often reward it with loyalty.

• Focus on Relationships
Rather than focusing on a single sale, aim for long-term connections. This reduces the urge to take unethical shortcuts.

- **Empower the Buyer**

Respect your client's timeline. Offer honest guidance and let them decide when they are ready to purchase.

- **Choose the Right Culture**

Work with organisations that value integrity. If your workplace pushes you to behave unethically, ask yourself if you belong there.

- **Know the Rules**

Understand the laws and standards that apply to your industry. Being well-informed helps you stay on the right path.

Balancing Ambition and Integrity

Sales can be exciting, but the race to reach quotas can challenge your values. Is it worth harming your reputation just to hit a number? Success earned ethically lasts longer because it is built on genuine trust and respect. When you look after your client's interests, you prove you are reliable and honest. This increases the chances of repeat business and positive word-of-mouth.

- **Build Real Relationships**

People buy from those they trust. If you know your customer's goals and work to meet them, your connections will be stronger and more profitable over time.

- **Set Clear Boundaries**

Refuse to oversell or lie about your products. Walking away from a shady deal can protect your good name.

- **Align Your Goals with Your Values**

If your employer demands unethical behaviour, consider speaking up or finding a better environment. A culture that respects honesty will help you thrive.

- **Use a Consultative Approach**

Guide customers by understanding their problems and offering the right solutions. This reduces pressure on both sides and avoids manipulative tactics.

- **Think Long Term**

Every ethical action helps create your personal brand. If people see you as fair and honest, they will be more likely to keep working with you.

Leading by Example

Have you ever considered how your choices might influence others on your team or across the industry? When you negotiate ethically, you set a positive example. Clients notice when you are open about costs or admit that another company's product might suit them better. Such openness can actually strengthen your credibility.

Leaders have a duty to train and guide their teams toward honesty. A supportive environment encourages team members to bring up tricky situations and discuss them without fear. This kind of culture allows everyone to learn from each other and avoid unethical shortcuts.

By choosing integrity, you show that sales can be both profitable and principled. You may face pressure to cut corners, but doing the right thing often earns more trust, more repeat customers and more referrals. In the end, ethical negotiation is not just about being good—it is also about being successful for the long haul.

24. Refining Your Skills: Continuous Learning and Improvement

In the fast-paced world of sales, closing a deal is important—but the real learning often comes afterwards. Have you ever stopped to think about how you handled a negotiation once it was over? This moment of self-reflection is key to growing your skills. By looking back on what went right and what went wrong, you turn each negotiation into a chance to get better.

Start by thinking about your successes. Did you make a genuine connection with the other person? Did you ask the right questions to discover what they needed? Notice what strategies worked well for you. For instance, if you linked your product to the customer's biggest problem and saw a positive reaction, remember that approach. Celebrating your strengths will help you use them more often in the future.

Next, be honest about where you struggled. Did the conversation get stuck at a certain point? Did strong emotions affect your thinking? These moments can be hard to face, but they teach you the most. Write them down and create an action plan. For example, if you had trouble talking about price, you might learn some new ways to show the product's value or adjust how you present your offer.

It also helps to reflect on how well you prepared. Did you learn enough about your customer's market, competitors and goals before the meeting? If not, plan to spend more time on research next time. Gathering the right information helps you feel more confident and offer better solutions.

Finally, try to get feedback from others. You could ask a trusted colleague or even the customer for their honest opinion. A fresh point of view may reveal areas you overlooked. By reflecting on every win and loss, you will grow stronger with each deal, gaining an edge in the highly competitive sales environment.

Seeking Feedback to Sharpen Negotiation Skills

Feedback is one of the most helpful tools for improving in sales, yet many people do not use it enough. In IT sales, where the pressure to close deals is very high, learning from each negotiation can be the difference between staying the same and becoming a master negotiator.

Feedback from Customers
After you finish a negotiation, consider asking the customer for feedback. A simple question, such as, "Is there anything I could have done better to meet your expectations?" can open the door to useful insights. Customers may point out parts of your pitch that did not match their goals or times when you missed an important worry they had. Taking their comments to heart will help you adjust your approach for future meetings.

Feedback from Peers
Your sales team is often a great source of advice. They have faced similar deals and can offer a different point of view. Role-playing with teammates can help you test new strategies in a safe space. A peer might notice that you need to use deeper questions or choose stronger closing statements. By

supporting each other, you not only grow as individuals but also build a stronger team.

Feedback from Managers
Managers have a wide view of the entire sales process. They often spot patterns you may not see, such as relying too much on discounts or stumbling over objections about price. Regular one-on-one sessions with them should focus on how you achieved your results, not just the results themselves. Taking this advice on board shows that you want to learn and adapt.

Seeking feedback from these three groups—customers, peers and managers—can transform each negotiation into a valuable lesson. Over time, your growing skills will help you succeed in the most challenging sales roles.

Staying Updated on Negotiation Trends

Sales is always changing and staying updated on new negotiation techniques is not just useful—it is necessary. Buyer behaviour shifts, new tools become available and market conditions evolve. If you do not keep up, you could be left behind.

Some modern negotiation tactics are shaped by changing buyer psychology and the rise of data-driven solutions. For example, value-based selling focuses on matching your product to the buyer's specific needs instead of just competing on price. Tools like Power BI allow you to use data to build a stronger argument. If you fail to track these changes, someone else might win deals by offering solutions that speak directly to what buyers want.

Keep in mind that buyers today often do their own research online before speaking to you. They come with certain expectations and a clear sense of what they need. This means you must be equally prepared. Bringing insight and knowledge to the table helps you stand out and gain their trust.

Shifts in the economy and technology can also affect how people make decisions. For example, the rise of artificial intelligence and automation has changed many buying processes. If you stay alert to these changes and update your approach, you will remain relevant—and even lead the way.

The Power of Role-Play

Role-playing is a great way to improve negotiation skills, especially in high-pressure sales roles. It allows you to practise real scenarios without the risk of losing an actual deal. The key is to make these exercises as close to real life as possible.

First, choose situations that your team often faces. For instance, if you sell IT services, focus on how to handle price objections, multi-level decision-makers, or doubts about new technologies. Use examples from past deals to make it feel realistic.

Then, set clear goals for your role-play. Are you practising how to handle a certain objection? Or do you want to sharpen your closing style? Focus on one or two aims so everyone knows what they are working on.

Assign roles carefully. One person acts as the salesperson, while the other plays the customer. Give the "customer" a detailed story, including their top needs and possible worries. Add surprises like sudden changes in the budget or a last-minute objection. These twists feel real and prepare you for anything that might happen with a real customer.

After the role-play, spend time on feedback. Look at what went well and what needs work. If someone calmly turned a price objection into a discussion about return on investment (ROI), highlight this win. By repeating these exercises with new angles, everyone builds confidence and quick thinking for real negotiations.

Building Your Personal Development Plan (PDP)

In sales, negotiation skills are at the heart of your success, but many people forget to develop them on purpose. Creating a Personal Development Plan (PDP) focused on negotiation can help you stay ahead in this competitive field. How do you start?

First, set clear goals. Instead of saying, "I want to be better at negotiating," be specific. Perhaps aim to close three major deals by using advanced negotiation methods or reduce discounts by 20% through stronger pricing talks. Precise targets make it easier to measure your growth.

Next, take a close look at your strengths and weaknesses. Do you connect well with people but stumble when talking about money? Or do you handle objections easily but find it hard to show the true value of your product? Identifying these areas helps you focus your energy where it is needed most.

Then, map out simple steps to achieve your goals. You might decide to read a top negotiation book, like *Never Split the Difference* by Chris Voss. You could attend a webinar or sign up for a workshop. You can also practise these ideas by role-playing with a colleague.

Feedback is key, so do not forget to ask for it after each major negotiation. What worked well and what did not? How can you adjust? Keep track of your progress with numbers, such as how many deals you close or how many new clients renew their contracts. Celebrate small successes, but do not stop improving. Negotiation is an art that grows with each new experience.

By creating and following a PDP, you take control of your career and show that you are serious about becoming a top performer. In today's fast-paced sales jobs, that extra edge can make all the difference.

25. Conclusion: Mastering Negotiation for Sales Success

Mastery in negotiation is not a final destination. It is a journey that goes on and on. This journey requires continuous effort, conscious practise and a strong desire to learn from every interaction. For those who work in the demanding world of sales, where targets are high and competitors seek the same deals, strong negotiation skills can be the key to moving from average results to true success.

This book explores the main ideas behind effective negotiation. First, it looks at the mindset you need to excel. Confidence, empathy and flexibility are crucial traits, yet they are often learned through experience rather than inherited. Here, you will discover the power of preparation—researching prospects, finding out what motivates them and planning for objections. Good preparation is not just a step in the process; it is the solid base that sets experts apart from beginners.

Next, we focus on communication. This includes both what you say and how you say it without words. We will discuss techniques like active listening, strategic questioning and noticing non-verbal signals. Great negotiators do not just speak; they pay attention, make adjustments and skilfully guide the discussion.

Of course, the path is not always smooth. You may face challenges such as handling rejection or working with difficult personalities. You may also feel the pressure of a high-stakes sales role. Throughout this book, you will find real-life stories and practical tips that help you overcome these obstacles. With the right approach, you can turn problems into chances to learn.

Above all, this book reminds you that mastery is not a natural gift but the result of hard work. Every call, meeting and deal offers a chance to improve. Negotiation mastery is a craft, much like painting or carpentry. It needs patience, persistence and the bravery to keep going even when results are not instant.

If you are ready to commit to this path, the rewards can be huge. You will feel more confident, build stronger connections and close deals that others only dream about.

Sales may feel like a battlefield at times. Yet real success does not come from how many calls you make or how many deals you try to rush through. It comes from preparing well, listening actively and giving your customers what they truly need. Here are the 25.2 key lessons this book highlights:

- **Preparation is Everything**
Always start with thorough research. Learn about your client's business, uncover their biggest challenges and shape your offer to match their goals. Go beyond one-size-fits-all solutions and craft unique ideas that truly connect.

- **Master Active Listening**

Many salespeople talk too much. Instead, focus on listening. Ask open-ended questions that bring hidden needs into the light. Reflect these points back to your client to show you understand. Often, your greatest strength is how well you grasp their real issues.

- **Create Value Beyond Price**

Competing on price alone leads to lower and lower profit. Instead, highlight the extra value of your solution. Use examples, client success stories and return-on-investment figures to show how you solve their problems better than anyone else.

- **Build Relationships, Not Transactions**

Long-term success comes from honest connections. Be genuine, stay in touch regularly and notice small details that matter to the client. When you build trust and respect, you get repeat business and referrals.

- **Leverage Data and Metrics**

Tools like Power BI can help you study trends and spot new openings. When you use data wisely, your sales pitches become more convincing and more precise.

- **Adapt and Persevere**

Sales can be tough, but it also teaches you to be resilient. Learn from rejections, adjust your approach and keep coming back stronger.

Remember, the ".2" takeaway is that you should always leave space to improve. No matter how skilled you are, the best salespeople never stop learning.

Yet negotiation skills are not limited to selling. In fact, they are useful in many parts of everyday life. Whether you are at work, at home, or socialising with friends, the core ideas of negotiation—understanding needs, promoting teamwork and aiming for mutually beneficial results—can make your relationships stronger and your interactions smoother.

In the workplace, negotiation goes beyond meeting with clients. It appears when you discuss tasks with your team, when you manage projects and even when you are planning your career. For example, if you are a manager trying to set deadlines, you need to balance company goals with your team's welfare. By listening carefully and suggesting flexible solutions, you can meet both the organisation's targets and the team's workload limits, boosting morale and productivity. Likewise, asking for a pay rise or promotion also relies on explaining your value, seeing the company's point of view and tackling their doubts. These are the same principles used in sales negotiations.

At home, negotiation often appears in family planning. For instance, deciding where to go on holiday might require finding common ground on budget, location and activities. Just like in business, aiming for a win-win result and keeping communication open helps everyone feel included.

Negotiation can also calm conflict. Whether you are trying to settle a disagreement with a co-worker or a family member, taking a confrontational approach can make things worse. Instead, think of disagreements as chances to collaborate. This mindset builds trust and improves relationships.

If you are in a high-pressure sales job, remember that negotiation is not just a professional skill; it is also a life skill. It allows you to find harmony, fix problems and create strong connections, no matter the situation. By using these ideas in all areas of your life, you will not only excel in your career but also grow on a personal level.

Negotiation is both an art and a science. It is a lifelong journey. For those working in fast-paced sales roles, negotiations can feel like do-or-die battles. Deals hang in the balance and the pressure can be intense. However, the truth is that great negotiators are not born. They become skilled through steady practise, determination and a strong will to keep growing.

Your mindset is where the journey begins. Negotiation is not about defeating the other side. It is about building value, earning trust and finding answers that work for everyone. This simple change in thinking is vital. Do not look at the other person as your enemy. Instead, see them as your partner. Aim for solutions that benefit both sides so you can build lasting bonds, not just short-term deals.

Of course, real-life experience is your greatest teacher. Yet you must reflect on your wins and losses to turn those experiences into expertise. After each negotiation, ask yourself: *What went well?* *What could I have done differently?* This habit of self-reflection keeps you learning and improving.

Being flexible is also important. Markets change, customers change and what worked last month might not work today. Stay curious. Read articles, study new strategies and ask for advice from mentors and colleagues. Stagnation is the biggest enemy of excellence.

Remember that negotiation does not stand alone. It is made up of many skills, like being aware of your own emotions and those of others, listening actively, speaking clearly and thinking strategically. Strengthen each of these pieces and your power in negotiations will soar.

Becoming a great negotiator never truly ends. It is an ongoing path that rewards those who face its challenges with an open mind, a willingness to work hard and the commitment to keep getting better.

In this book, you have discovered ways to succeed in high-pressure sales. You have seen how to meet demanding targets while protecting your mental health. You have learnt how to build resilience and sharpen your negotiation skills. Now it is time to put these lessons into action.

Start by focusing on small, steady improvements. Sales victories are not built overnight. They are earned through persistence, discipline and the ability to adapt. Try setting clear, manageable goals for what you want to improve. Perhaps you want to refine how you find new clients, polish your presentation, or strengthen your follow-up routine. Track your progress and celebrate small wins. Each success encourages you to aim higher.

Also, do not do it alone. Look for mentors and peers who understand what you are going through. Let them challenge you to grow while offering support when things get tough.

Keep learning, too. The sales world changes all the time and you need to keep pace by staying a student. Read industry blogs, listen to podcasts and sign up for online courses. I highly recommend *Never Split the Difference* by Chris Voss for further negotiation tips and *Fanatical Prospecting* by Jeb Blount to improve your outreach efforts.

Finally, remember to care for your mental and physical health. Sales is a marathon, not a sprint. No deal is worth harming your well-being.

You have amazing potential and your growth starts with your decision to move forward. The next chapter of your success story is in your hands—go and make it remarkable.

Printed in Great Britain
by Amazon

Copyright Notice

© 2025 Aidan Dickenson

Rights Reserved Notice

All rights reserved. No part of this publication may be reproduced, stored in a retrieval system, or transmitted in any form by any means—electronic, mechanical, photocopying, recording, or otherwise—without prior written permission from the copyright holder.

This publication is provided for general informational purposes only and should not be relied upon as a substitute for professional advice. Every effort has been made to ensure accuracy at the time of printing, but the author and publisher shall not be held liable for any errors or omissions, or for any outcomes related to the use of this content.

The material in this book is not intended to serve as legal, financial, medical, or other professional guidance. Readers are encouraged to seek tailored advice from qualified professionals concerning specific matters relevant to their individual circumstances.

The opinions expressed in this publication are those of the author and do not necessarily reflect the views of any organisations, institutions, or companies that may be referenced. Examples used herein are for illustrative purposes only and should not be interpreted as endorsements.

References to product names, trademarks and registered marks are for identification and information purposes only. All such trademarks remain the property of their respective owners and no affiliation with or endorsement by these owners is implied.